spilt milk

linda vujnov

devotions for moms

spilt milk

ZONDERVAN®

ZONDERVAN.com/
AUTHORTRACKER
follow your favorite authors

ZONDERVAN

Spilt Milk
Copyright © 2009 by Linda Vujnov

Requests for information should be addressed to:
Zondervan, *Grand Rapids, Michigan 49530*

Library of Congress Cataloging-in-Publication Data

Vujnov, Linda, 1963-
  Spilt milk : devotions for moms / Linda Vujnov.
    p. cm.
  ISBN 978-0-310-28511-3 (softcover)
  1. Mothers — Prayers and devotions. I. Title.
BV4847.V85 2008
242'.6431 — dc22   2008040322

Interior design by Christine Orejuela-Winkelman

Printed in the United States of America

---

09 10 11 12 13 14 • 20 19 18 17 16 15 14 13 12 11 10 9 8 7 6 5 4 3 2 1

To God, whose grace and mercy overwhelm me
and who deserves all glory and honor.

To my biggest fan and supporter, my rock, Greg,
who took the children on three-hour "field trips"
so I could finish my manuscript.

contents

dead yet

"Is she dead yet?" I asked, shuffling past my son and daughter as they burst into the seventeenth performance of a silly, hand-clappy, nonsensical melody about a gal named Miss Susie. The lyrics start when Miss Susie is a baby, giving childish details as to what Miss Susie says through each milestone of her life.

It goes something like this: "Miss Susie was a baby, a baby, a baby, Miss Susie was a baby, she went like this, "Where's my bottle?" The singsong continues along with questions she asks, depending on her age. The final line is, "Miss Susie was a grandma, a grandma, a grandma, Miss Susie was a grandma, and she went like this, "Where's my cane?"

As day turned to night, the song became more incessant and irritating. Who in the world is Miss Susie, and why would anyone create such an annoying rhyming song about her? My two oldest children spent the next twenty-four plus hours facing each other in different parts of every room, slapping hands and chanting about this strange character named Miss Susie. This insidious clang, clang, rubbish, quickly became impressed on my brain.

I caught myself while in the shower or feeding the dog or doing laundry repeating Miss Susie's life story — ugh! Only severe drugs could clear the mentally etched song. Why did I remember a song about Miss Susie, whom I don't even know, but I cannot seem to remember a Scripture past the first reading?

The best way to remember Scripture is by repeating it over and over again. We, as believers, need to make Scripture memory a part of our daily quiet time. Easier said than done? Of course! But there is one thing that is for sure: it takes one step to start the journey. Standing still will get you nowhere.

At the end of each *Spilt Milk* devotion I include a Scripture verse. Feel free to sing them to yourself to the tune of "Mary Had a Little Lamb" or the *Little Einsteins* theme song — whatever it takes to get them stuck in your head like Miss Susie's still stuck in mine, although by now she must be dead.

For those of you who cannot carry a tune past your

front door, are in the church choir but shouldn't be, or (like me) would end up in the outtakes of *American Idol*, don't fret. Another way to get Scriptures stuck in your head is to write them on sticky notes and adhere them to bathroom mirrors, the refrigerator, the pantry, or wherever you visit during your daily routine. Oh, by the way. I don't recommend sticking one to your two-year-old's forehead. It keeps falling off.

> *I have hidden your word in my heart*
> *that I might not sin against you.*
>> *Psalm 119:11*

donuts and marbled rye

Saturday morning was quite possibly the most exciting day of the week in my neighborhood as I was growing up. This day marked the arrival of the Helms truck, whose two-toned exterior could be seen for miles. Its unique whistle rustled up sleepy-eyed families, luring them curbside in order to satisfy their taste buds with "fresh from the oven" donuts, pastries, and sliced loaves of bread.

My older brother and I would run out our front door, stand on the edge of our driveway, and wave our hands above our heads, signaling the driver to stop in front of our house. My dad slowly trickled out behind us, clutching his wallet and readjusting the belt of his robe.

A friendly man dressed in white pants and a button-down

white shirt would stop the truck so that our bodies were perfectly aligned with the end of his back bumper. He would throw open the back door of the truck, which would then emit an aromatic cocktail of sugar, yeast, and butter. He pulled out wide, flat drawers and exposed an array of every flavor of pastry and donut imaginable, while steaming loaves of bread were seen tucked neatly in the center section of the truck.

Hundreds of choices meant that time ticked slowly for the deliveryman. He patiently waited as we gazed at the treasure trove sitting among us. The admonition to "choose just one" was an excruciatingly difficult task for two small children. Even after my dad had picked out the perfect loaf of marbled rye bread and his usual jelly donut, we remained undecided. The selection was overwhelming, although any decision would have been perfect.

Dad paid the tab, while we slowly returned to the porch, nibbling our fare. As we savored each bite, we promised ourselves that next Saturday we would try a different pastry, in the gluttonous hope of eventually experiencing every offering.

What if I were to purchase a pastry, walk inside the house, and place it on a shelf and leave it there? Ludicrous! Eventually it would get stale, lose its flavor, be deemed unfit, and be subjected to the garbage can. The sole purpose of a donut is to tantalize taste buds while causing feelings of dreaminess and pure delight. The sugar crash and additional cellulite come much later.

All of us have gifts — talents that God wants us to share with others. While many of us desire to be great wives and mothers, we often squelch our talents and gifts as we assume that our selfish desires would be fed if we used these to benefit ourselves and others.

In the utmost ragtag interpretation of Greek, God calls this ludicrous. His face beams with pride when we honor him by using the gifts he has given in order to help others and further his kingdom. There is a spring in his step when we are doing his will for our lives, and his penetrating smile lights up the heavens as he watches us commit to his purpose.

Even though our bodies are made up of many parts, they work together for one good. We are the body of Christ, called to use our gifts and talents whenever we can. If you are musical, sing for others. If you are creative, design a flyer for your child's school. If you love helping with the elderly, volunteer at your local senior center. If you delight in home organization, come to my house! Dig deep, discover that which brings you joy, the talent in which you delight.

The Helms truck went out of business when grocery stores began selling fresh baked goods at a cheaper price. Although I still crave the warm pastries that were delivered each Saturday morning to our doorstep, my current quest is locating the perfect cinnamon roll — warm, moist, gooey, and coated with velvety icing (sans the raisins).

spilt milk

There are different kinds of gifts, but the same Spirit distributes them. There are different kinds of service, but the same Lord. There are different kinds of working, but in all of them and in everyone it is the same God at work.

1 Corinthians 12:4–6

oh BGYN

Recently I had a well-woman appointment at the gynecologist, which is strange since there is nothing "well-woman" about the fact that I feel like my uterus is dragging between my ankles.

Although I'm not into small talk while sitting naked wearing only a tissue-paper poncho and covered with a butcher-paper blanket, forty-five minutes or so alone without clamoring children and armed with a book and fashion magazine was the "bright side" of my situation.

I grinned as I walked down the hall, realizing I was five minutes early. As I opened the door to the doctor's office, I got hit with the time management reality stick. Of the twelve chairs crammed into this closet laughingly called a waiting room, there were ten people and one stroller. My disappointment surfaced, and my smile sunk.

Squeezing my way to the check-in clipboard, I began filling in the necessities. While writing down my scheduled appointment time, I noticed that I was one of four people with a 9:40 appointment with the same doctor. Letting out a frustrated moan, I maneuvered through legs and feet, sat, and began reading my magazine.

After flipping through my magazine at record speed, I decided the book I chose was going to need live animals and circus performers to suddenly burst forth from the pages in order to keep my attention. My boredom gauge nearly spun off the dial after thirty-nine minutes of waiting, and the air felt thick enough to chew.

Chatty Cathy and her friend Carla sat behind the glass window, seemingly oblivious to our miserable situation, carrying on with their filing and phone-answering duties, avoiding the glass window entirely. People continued to enter the waiting room, and only a few exited, forcing a "standing room only" situation.

Glancing at my watch, I realized that I had been waiting for an unacceptable one hour and ten minutes. I rehearsed in my mind the spewing sarcastic comments I would unleash to the gals behind the glass enclosure. As I began huffing and puffing my way to the window, "Cathy" must have noticed the flames coming out of my ears and said, "They're calling you back right now."

I quickly collected my belongings and felt a gust of arrogance as I looked back at those still waiting. The nurse and I meandered through small talk while walking toward the scale. My happy face was in full bloom since I was now on the *other* side of the door. She walked me to a closed door, and as she attempted to stick my file in the holder attached to the door, she realized there was already a file placed inside.

Someone was still in the room, and all of the rooms were still occupied.

As she apologized and escorted me back to the waiting room, I felt as though I was in one of those black-and-white horror movies where the giant, hairy ant is attacking the woman and grabbing her face as the woman screams and shakes her head — "No! No!" — all the while backing up and continuing to scream with disbelief.

As I reluctantly returned to the waiting room, I hurled my haughtiness under the chair and attempted to find a seat. People began staring at me, wondering what sin I must have committed in order to be sent back to purgatory. Just as I was ready to spew every cussword I knew at the "gyno gals," I remembered something that I had read in the book of James about controlling the tongue: "And so blessing and cursing come pouring out of the same mouth. Surely, my brothers and sisters, this is not right!" (James 3:10 NLT).

It was then that I took a cleansing breath, stuffed my

cusswords into my back pocket, bit my tongue, and called my mother to let her know that I would be picking up the kids sometime next week.

Letting Scriptures sit in my mind unused and unmoving is not enough for me. When I read God's Word, I need to apply what it says to my daily life. I need to deliberately carry out what God instructs me to do as a Christian woman, although there may be a large degree of difficulty. Inevitably I will mess up and make mistakes. However, with the guidance of God's Word I can do a better job of following what he commands.

My little postcard arrived, informing me that the time has come for my next well-woman appointment. I went ahead and scheduled the appointment for 10:15, but this time I'll be more prepared. I'm packing my sleeping bag, pillow, coffeepot, sack lunch, portable DVD player, and an array of books, including my Bible — just in case I have to wait.

Therefore, as God's chosen people, holy and dearly loved, clothe yourselves with compassion, kindness, humility, gentleness and patience.

Colossians 3:12

a single dad

In my home, Joseph of Nazareth became a widower. This catastrophe occurred when my two-year-old attempted to snuggle with Mary from our nativity scene and dropped her on the tile floor, instantly decapitating her. Tile and porcelain do not mix.

As I swept the debris, I tried to imagine how different Jesus' life would have been if Mary's life had been cut short. Which lessons would have gone unlearned if she hadn't been around for the raising of Jesus? There would have been no one to gently caution him to get off of the stable roof. Dads are usually the ones who tell the boys to climb a little higher.

spilt milk

When the time came for him to start school, Mary would not be there to pack his lunch and include the characteristic "Happy first day of school!" note. Let's talk art projects for a minute. Who would lovingly admire his dead lizard collage created in the desert sand? Only a mother could see the artistic imagery in a creation of that caliber.

The laundry would be a whole other issue. He would soon discover that a white robe and a red robe are never washed in the same basin. The bread would be flat, the sandals left in the living room, and the beds unmade. However, he would probably be the first on his block to pop a wheelie in his donkey cart, and his water-to-wine science project would blow away all of the other sixth graders.

Unfortunately, there are children who do not have the luxury of learning life's lessons in a two-parent home. For a myriad of reasons, families are missing either a mother or a father. Many of them are physically missing, while others have simply checked out mentally. Women all over the world are being forced to assume the role of both mother and father.

In these circumstances, comfort comes from knowing that we are not alone in our struggle to accomplish an impossible task. We have a Father in heaven who steps in at any given moment to help us through difficult or trying situations when we ask. By placing God first in our lives, we will be better mothers and better modelers of Jesus' love. By surrendering to him, we allow his work to be done.

In moments that seem overwhelming, we must remember that God loves us and is walking by our side every step of the way. He promises to never give us more than we can handle.

*Cast your cares on the L*ORD
    and he will sustain you;
he will never let
    the righteous be shaken.
                              Psalm 55:22

FOLA JOY

Vanity plates are rampant in my county. Everything from a SUV bearing MOMOF10 to LGLDUDE to a compact car with FAUX CUS has graced our highways and byways. For the vanity plate-challenged, I have on occasion seen drivers print the translation on the frame that secures the plate to the automobile — as a cheat sheet.

One plate in particular caught my eye as I was careening over for a lane change. An older, paint-chipped white Mercedes was wearing a plate with the letters FOLA JOY. Whenever I catch a glimpse of a personalized plate, the game is to try and solve the letter puzzle before the car speeds out of view. Repeating the letters in my head brought the "aha!" and the pieces were in place: full of joy. Not necessarily my first choice in personalized plates.

Thinking through the type of plate I'd have on my car began a game. Given that circumstances and emotions change as the second hand on a clock, I decided I would need three or four plates that could be switched to coincide with my present mood or situation. NEEDSLEEP, 2MNYKIDS, FOLA ANGST, and DINNER IDEAS NE1 did not suitably fit into the seven-letter legal format so they were instantly eliminated.

On the way to work, I pondered the thought *full of joy*. How great to be full of joy! How proud God would feel to see his children full of joy! Galatians 5:22–23 came to mind. "The fruit of the Spirit is love, joy, peace, patience, kindness, goodness, faithfulness, gentleness and self-control."

How many of us could bear the vanity plate that shouted to the world, "full of love"? How about "full of peace?" Maybe this one: "full of goodness?" How many? Very few.

Not me.

Self-centeredness is effortless. Jealousy and outbursts of anger come easily. Try as I might, those hideous character flaws sneak into my day and rear their ugly heads. Constant prayer and effort are the only way to combat my sinful nature. When we allow the Holy Spirit to control our lives, good fruit is produced.

Often I start off pleading with God to fill me with the ability to show godly behavior, but one way or another, human nature and reaction intervene quite quickly, and BOOM! — I am back on my knees. I have blown it once again.

God does not expect me to get it right every time. What a relief! However, my actions need to demonstrate the fact that I am a Christian. I do know this: when I spend time in God's Word and pray often, I'm better able to demonstrate Christlike characteristics.

With God's help I can be FOLA JOY — even FOLA PATIENCE. As the 70s bumper sticker says, "Please be patient. God isn't finished with me yet" — and he won't be finished until I enter eternity.

Be joyful in hope, patient in affliction, faithful in prayer.

Romans 12:12

brotherly loathe

I am sure that during our childhood my parents wondered if my brother and I would ever love each other — let alone be friends — because most of the injuries I endured as a child were caused by my older brother. I guess there is some sick humor in watching your little sister cry.

Once, I was riding on the handlebars of my brother's Schwinn Sting-Ray bike. The handlebars made a deep "U" shape, which fit my bottom perfectly. He coerced me into agreeing by assuring me that this would be great fun. The "fun" ended in blood and tears as my bare foot met some unrelenting spokes, which propelled me off the handlebars in a frontal dismount that should have landed me a gold medal — but instead gave me a broken arm.

Another "fun" idea that went awry, for me at least,

occurred during a motorcycle ride in a vacant field behind my dad's office. My brother sweet-talked me into riding on the back of the motorcycle by promising that he would not pop a wheelie. I trustingly mounted the motorcycle, wrapped my arms securely around his waist, and off we went. My joy came to an abrupt end when he popped a wheelie, and I landed on the dirt with a thud. My reward for trusting my brother was a mouth full of dirt and a head full of hurt. Being gullible has consequences.

Another one of his favorite tease techniques was to pin me down with his bony knees, restricting all movement and eliminating any hope of escape. He would then proceed to conjure up a loogie, followed by a slow release that allowed the slime to dangle above my screaming face. At the last possible moment, he would slurp it up and fall backward in hysterical laughter. I failed to see the humor.

Since I was the "world's best tattletale," his injury-causing escapades never went unreported to my parents. After all, isn't that in the job description of a little sister?

My brother's teasing was sometimes so relentless that there were moments when I thought that, if given the opportunity, he would have sold me into slavery. It's a good thing for me that we weren't alive in biblical times.

The Bible recounts an event where men actually did sell their sibling into slavery. His name was Joseph. He was the golden child. His dad Jacob loved him so much that he gave him a beautiful robe, purchased from Dolce & Gabbana on Rodeo Drive and ornamented with Cartier and Tiffany diamonds. This caused his brothers to be so jealous that they wanted him dead.

Instead, they eliminated their problem by selling him to a caravan of Midianite merchants, minus the robe. They should have returned the robe to Dolce & Gabbana and split the money evenly, but in order to cover up the horrendous act of selling off Joseph, they rubbed his robe with goat's blood and told their father he had been devoured by a ferocious beast. This was, of course, before DNA testing.

Indisputably, an extreme case of brotherly loathing.

Joseph could have spent his life hating his brothers for what they did; instead he knew that what they meant for evil, God meant for good. Therefore, when Joseph had the opportunity to help his brothers and their families, he didn't hesitate. He showed how much he loved them by giving them everything they needed.

In spite of all of the torture I tolerated at my brother's hand, I am happy to report that his subtle attempts to destroy my psyche failed, and I am a reasonably well-adjusted adult. What's more, we are good friends and love each other. Still, even though he outweighs me, I'm sure I could easily take him down, render him immobile with my bony knees, and conjure up a loogie — if I had to.

Dear friends, let us love one another, for love comes from God. Everyone who loves has been born of God and knows God. Whoever does not love does not know God, because God is love.

1 John 4:7−8

pishaw delivery awe

I could smell the chutzpah surrounding the car from twenty-five yards away. The shiny sticker on the back window read "Single and Beautiful." My eyes darted around the neighborhood, hoping to catch a glimpse of this bold beauty, but to my chagrin, she never emerged from the nearby homes.

When I was young and single, the popular license plate frame for gals with gall was "So many men, so little time." As a college junior with a self-deprecating sense of humor, I personalized my license plate frame with the phrase "So much time, so few men" and wore a button on my backpack that stated, "Boyfriend wanted. Applications now being accepted." Although my "in-box" was not teetering with a tower of applications, and cute boys weren't stopping me on the street offering me dinner and a movie, I was able to rustle up a boy to escort me to a dance at school without having to pay him large sums of money.

My girlfriend and I decided to entertain our dates with dinner, and we figured that my cozy bungalow would serve as the perfect location since it sat only a few yards from the sand on the bay side of the Pacific Ocean.

With the guarantee of a gourmet dinner cleverly named "Pishaw Delivery Awe," our dates arrived, expecting exotic aromas to assault their senses. Instead, they experienced "take and bake" pizza, delivered by my 1978 Volkswagen Bug. Our fancy French cuisine was a complete fake, and the only thing missing was a hidden camera and a producer jumping out from behind a curtain yelling, "Gotcha!"

Nevertheless, we enjoyed the fare and laughed about the meal and explained to our dates that two girls, consumed with priming and primping for a dance, were unable to cook a meal too. Thankfully our dates understood.

Jacob, from the book of Genesis, was the king of "faking it." While Isaac, Jacob's father, was dying and his vision was askew, he asked his oldest son, Esau, to hunt some game and prepare a meal. Isaac then instructed him to come by his side in order that he may receive a blessing from him before he died — the blessing meant for the firstborn. Esau went to carry out his father's request.

Upon hearing this secret information, Jacob's mother, Rebekah, coaxed Jacob into deceiving Isaac and stealing the blessing from Esau. Rebekah favored Jacob and wanted the blessing for him. Jacob dressed in his brother's clothing, prepared a feast for his father, covered his arms with goatskins to appear hairy like his brother, and stole his brother's blessing. He swindled his own father in order to reap the blessing that was meant for Esau.

There were no cameras that appeared in that scene either. This was faultless fraud. Isaac was hoodwinked, and there was no correcting what had just gone wrong. The blessing was gone, used up on the wrong person — a con artist in goats' fur.

God worked out his will in spite of the sins of Rebekah and Jacob. Even though Esau hated his brother and plotted to kill him, God's grace was at work behind the scene. In spite of the sin, in spite of the hatred, in spite of the deception, God would continue to love and bless the life of Jacob. God's grace abounds.

There are no hurt feelings when I serve the French delicacy Pishaw Delivery Awe to my family. The repercussions include everyone squealing with delight when the cardboard box arrives and paper plates are left empty. This particular cuisine has become a midweek dinner staple. However, I'm working on a new entrée that also happens to be French. It's called Toquet Away Cheeneez. This dish comes complete with folded cookies for dessert, and the cleanup is a breeze. I have become quite the gourmet cook.

The wisdom of the prudent is to give thought to their ways,
but the folly of fools is deception.

Proverbs 14:8

idiot alert

"All men are idiots, and I married the king of them." I was stunned as I read the license plate frame while leaving the grocery store. Although I had a few ideas of my own for a personal license plate frame, this one wouldn't have made the list of options. The disrespect was pooling in the parking lot stall.

My husband is the first to admit that men are idiots, but he is a man. Although men are not perfect, they do a lot of things right. Who do you call when there is an abnormally large, fuzzy, creepy thing on your kitchen floor? Who is patient enough to move the couch at seven different angles while you stand, finger on chin, deciding which works best with your design scheme? And who, willingly, carries the toddlers on their shoulders during the grueling hikes around the church carnivals? Your guess is correct. Our men!

Television shows and movies have taken the liberty of portraying men as idiots. Grown men are shown at football games grunting persistently, sitting shirtless in snow flurries, their bodies painted like a canvas. Some men are portrayed as those who place more importance on a donut and a television show than on spending time with their families. Television sons and daughters everywhere shake their heads in amazement as to how their dads turned out to be so clueless and moronic. One commercial depicts a father who can't multiply 5 times 5. He keeps getting 26.

In the beginning of time, God created man in his own image and named him Adam. God quickly discovered that Adam needed some companionship after watching him sit around the garden naked, naming creatures all day. Genius God created all of the beasts of the fields and the birds of the air, but from Adam's own rib he formed "woman."

When Adam saw Eve for the first time, I don't imagine he rolled his eyes, drooped his shoulders, and sighed, "Yeah, she'll do. What do I name her?" Most likely he tripped over his tongue, grew sweaty, smiled, and gasped. I think the Hebrew translation reads, "He shouted to God, 'She's perfect! Can I keep her?'"

When we find a man who becomes our husband, wonderful things transpire. Not only does this man acquire new titles like husband, lover, and dad; he no doubt becomes our rock of Gibraltar, protector, best friend, and biggest fan. As wives, the importance of encouragement, respect, and support for these men whom we love should be forefront. Equally important is reminding them how much we love and need them.

A side responsibility that accompanies marriage is to never allow our husbands to paint their faces and run around half-naked at a football game or to let them install a television in every bathroom of the house.

At times men may act like idiots, but (thankfully) the bitter woman with the sarcastic license plate frame married the king of them. Thank goodness for us, he's taken!

Each one of you also must love his wife as he loves himself, and the wife must respect her husband.

Ephesians 5:33

my last drink

When temperatures rise and sweat pools join with adjoining sweat pools in unreachable nooks and crannies in the body and then drain like a waterfall down the entire length of the spine, emotions can explode like a singed thermometer.

During the first week in September, the temperature in southern California soared to triple digits. I took my four children to an outdoor mall, where we soon discovered the heat we were trying to escape was sitting motionless, nestled between the cement buildings. In order to escape the heat we dove into doorways where the refreshing air-conditioned atmosphere cooled us for a brief moment. Then we would unwillingly return to the thick outdoors, where even dogs didn't feel like walking.

In my frustration at the unrelenting heat, I barked at everyone who spoke. Kind words from others brought no change in attitude, and gentle answers were cemented into the sidewalk beneath my melting flip-flops. Hunger beckoned, yet nothing sounded good enough to eat. Everyone wanted to avoid me, yet none of the children were old enough to take the keys and drive themselves home or wealthy enough to hail a taxi.

Our hope of escape from the heat sat a few yards away inside a beautiful, new Target store. As we entered through sliding doors, a blast of cold air chilled the sweat covering our bodies and gave us instant relief. My mother volunteered to feed the children some snack bar delicacies while I slowly shopped, free from any and all children requesting toys and other unnecessary items. My attitude adjusted as I lingered in the aisles, nibbled on a nutrition bar, and sauntered through the store. My thirst became apparent as I chewed the last bite of my bar, so I quickly grabbed a bottle of spring water from the shelves and unscrewed the top, took a long drink, and placed it in the shopping cart.

Stopping in the tea section, I studied each box in the hope that a flavor would jump out and entice my palate. While in deep concentration, I reached into the cart, grabbed the bottle again, unscrewed the top, and took a swig. Aghast, I spat the contents onto the floor as I realized that I had unintentionally taken a drink of the Pine-Sol instead of spring water.

As I cleaned up the mess on the floor, still feeling the sting of Pine-Sol on my lips and tongue, I couldn't help but think that God was telling me I needed to sanitize my speech and alter my attitude. I don't think that Pine-Sol was the immediate answer, but who am I to question God's choice for a proverbial washing out of the mouth?

I would have preferred to open my Bible and have Proverbs 17:27 jump out and suction itself to my eyeballs: "Those who have knowledge use words with restraint, and those who have understanding are even-tempered."

Reading would have been less agonizing.

If I were writing Proverbs, I would have finished the verse for more clarity. "And those who do not use words with restraint and do not control their tempers will mistakenly drink Pine Sol and regret their caustic comebacks."

I returned to the snack area and grossed out all of the children with my story. After apologizing for my attitude and curt behavior, I ordered a cup of coffee to counteract the pine taste still lingering on my lips and gums. Eventually we returned to the suffocating heat — armed with large cups of ice water and frozen slushies.

After all, if the outdoor heat became intolerable, we could soak ourselves with slushies. I'm always thinking.

Do not let any unwholesome talk come out of your mouths, but only what is helpful for building others up according to their needs, that it may benefit those who listen.

Ephesians 4:29

necessary weeping

Drooling isn't necessary, but it always seems to happen to my two younger boys when the mail carrier delivers the latest edition of *Lego Club Magazine*. They then sit side by side, deciding which architectural masterpiece will be their next purchase. They each grab a pen — black in color, writes on anything, and comes off of nothing, which we've appropriately named "scary pen" — to mark their favorites.

Although I love the imagination that Legos draw from my children and the skill needed to create small boats, planes, and race cars, I loathe the gaping, open sores they leave when I step on them with my bare foot. As the smaller pieces get sucked up by my vacuum, the clacking sound sends a shiver down my spine. I fear that one day these treasures will kill my vacuum cleaner — and my entire family will die a slow, excruciating death from drowning in a sea of dog hair.

Since the younger children have yet to master proper assemblage of a box of Legos containing more than ten pieces, the big kids and I are left wearing the badge labeled "engineer." For someone who hates putting together puzzles, this is torture. Add to this party a bowl of coconut, mayonnaise, and fresh tomatoes; weather in the low twenties; and cockroaches meandering over my tables and chairs, and I will tell you every last sin that I have ever committed (as well as the sins of my husband and four best friends). Who needs truth serum?

The latest products I was coaxed into acquiring were a fire hovercraft with 274 pieces and a rescue helicopter with 249 pieces. I offered my oldest son first choice as to which one he wanted to assemble, which left me with the fire hovercraft. Prior to construction I popped two aspirin into my mouth, swallowed hard, grabbed a mug of hot coffee, turned the oscillation fan to level three, and began the execution. I practically needed a magnifying glass to find the smaller pieces, and my fingers felt as big as salami rolls when I attempted to snap the tiny flashlight and walkie-talkie into place.

After one hour and nineteen minutes, both the fire hovercraft and rescue helicopter were complete. Our butts and backs ached from hunching over the coffee table while sitting on small plastic stools. We were so completely miserable that all my son and I could do was hold each other and weep.

These molded montages are considered treasures by my young boys, even though they are the only toy I know that falls apart within two days. They are strictly for looking and not touching. Odd. Four- and six-year-olds do not take those instructions too seriously.

Like my young boys, I, too, hold certain treasures close to my heart. My Bible is copiously cluttered with underlines and notes that are personal and reflective. I treasure my photos, which sit in dark boxes hoping to eventually land on the pages of a creative scrapbook.

In Ecclesiastes, King Solomon tells the story of how he took it upon himself to acquire everything he could get his hands on in order to find pleasure. His treasures included houses, gold, silver, the most expensive denim jeans he could find on 5th Avenue, more flocks and herds than anyone in Jerusalem before him, and an imported stroller from Italy. In the end he discerned that these treasures did not bring him pleasure and that they were "meaningless, a chasing after the wind" (Ecclesiastes 2:11).

Humanly speaking, we tend to place more value on what we have instead of what we need, and what we need is a joyful relationship with our Father in heaven and surrendered dependence on him. Only he can fill the empty parts in our souls. He pours out to us his complete grace, love, and mercy instead of filling our closets, garages, and homes.

Stuff goes out of style, forgets how to fit, breaks down on the highway, gets stained and torn, makes its way to the curb as a donation, gathers cobwebs, no longer performs what it was made to do, and collects spills. However, Jesus never goes out of style, fits like a glove, picks us up when we break down, washes our stains with his blood, donates his grace each day, creates safety webs to catch us when we fall, continuously meets our needs and performs miracles in our lives, and generously spills out his love for us — which is far better than any Lego fire hovercraft.

> *"Do not store up for yourselves treasures on earth, where moth and rust destroy, and where thieves break in and steal. But store up for yourselves treasures in heaven, where moth and rust do not destroy, and where thieves do not break in and steal."*
>
> Matthew 6:19–20

crater face

No damaging scars were left, even though I was called Crater Face my first day of sixth grade. This was partly due to the fact that the only part of Crater Face that was accurate was face; there were no visible craters. I must have had the self-esteem of Tony Robbins on an overdose of compliments. Otherwise, I would have been suicidal.

Since children possess the uncanny ability to take the simplest name and concoct an unflattering version, which potentially can stick to a person for years, my husband and I gave much thought in naming each of our children. With grandiose ideas, we selected a presidents theme — beginning with a dog named Truman. We named our first three children Madison, Zachary, and Ty (Tyler on the birth certificate.) By child number four we threw up our hands, opened a book of baby names, and simply pointed. Cadfrawd was instantly eliminated. Next we came up with the idea of using the names of our first dog and the names of the first street we lived on as children, but Missy Carfax and Lola Saybrook sounded like Las Vegas showgirls. Since our fourth child was a boy, we settled on Carson. What teacher could mispronounce Carson?

When I was young, I wanted my name to be Sandy. We lived in Southern California, and to me, Sandy epitomized a long-haired, beachy girl with endless legs and golden skin who had a surfboard permanently attached under her arm. I envisioned a Sandy as someone who could walk into her algebra class wearing a bikini and no one would point and snicker at her. Such is not the case with a Linda.

However, if parents declined to name their children until the children could pick out their own names, the outcome could be catastrophic. Salesmen could be named Spider-man; police officers, SpongeBob SquarePants; and lawyers, Buzz Lightyear. Girls could have the same problem. Nurses could be named Polly Pocket; preschool teachers, Pretty Princess; and mail carriers, Cinderella. The upside is that the explanation of the origin of these names would make for interesting dinner conversations.

When we accept Jesus as our Savior, we not only reap the benefit of eternal life; God inscribes our name in the Lamb's book of life. He knows each one of us by name. Our name is significant to our heavenly Father.

Even though we thoughtfully chose the names of our children and were pretty satisfied we did well, I had a rude awakening one morning while I was serving breakfast to my hungry brood. Each child wanted to know how we decided on their names. My middle boy was quite disappointed when I explained that he was named after a president. With furrowed brow he said, "Why didn't you name me Star Wars Darth Vader Storm Trooper." Seconds later, the youngest chimed in with, "Yeah! And my name should be Snowboard Motorcycle Guy." I thought for a moment and replied, "Yes, and my name should be Sandy."

"Do not fear, for I have redeemed you;
I have summoned you by name; you are mine."

Isaiah 43:1

dodging baseballs

Double A baseball separates the men from the boys — maybe more appropriately, the nine-year-olds from the T-ball gang.

Third grade marks a milestone in a boy's baseball life, because he begins to pitch to his opponent, which causes every player to leave his sissy pants at home. For these young folks, the windup and delivery could result in a strike, a foul ball, a great hit, or a nasty bruise.

As these Little Leaguers know, they moved from T-ball, where the ball just sits anticipating a good whack, to coach-pitch, where the coach receives most of the bruising. Next is machine pitch, where the ball comes hard, fast, and in the same location every time. This leads to the pinnacle test of nerves known as "kid pitch," where the ball and the pitcher have minds of their own. This often results in the ball meeting some very tender body part — thigh, ribs, shoulder, ankle. On the flip side, just as in the pros, if you do happen to have some ball and thigh interaction, the result is a much-deserved walk to first base, some cheers from the stands, and the first base coach wiping your tears and giving your hair a good tousle.

By the time these "men" turn ten and reach triple A baseball, they have grown a chestful of hair, burly beards, thick muscles, and they have incredible tear-holding-back mechanisms. Though not quite ready for the pros, those who stick around are now crowding the plate, staring down the pitcher and almost daring that hard ball to come anywhere near their thin, polyester baseball pants. These guys aren't afraid of anything except girls.

Looking back through the years, I recognize that there have been times in my life when dodging baseballs was a full-time job. Though the balls looked less white and were missing the thick red stitching, hurling at me at breakneck speed were financial difficulties, job failures, marriage issues, sicknesses, stresses, feelings of being overwhelmed, and pregnancy problems.

At these times, I felt I needed God to be my catcher, standing not behind the plate but in front of me keeping me safe. But sometimes God allows us to get hit by what life throws at us, for he knows that without adversity we cannot become more like him. He yearns for us to run to him when we are hit by one of those fastball trials. He gathers us into his tender arms, soothingly cups his hands around our face, wipes away our tears, and applies an ice pack on the welts of life that have left a sore impression.

As a good coach, God tousles our hair and sends us running back into the game. The sting still makes us wince, but the scabs fall off over time.

As Paul wrote to the Romans, "We also glory in our sufferings, because we know that suffering produces perseverance; perseverance, character; and character, hope" (Romans 5:3–4). Hope is the result of our utter dependence on God.

The apostle Paul knew well what dodging baseballs was all about, and I'm pretty certain he never wore sissy pants.

I have fought the good fight, I have finished the race, I have kept the faith.

2 Timothy 4:7

time-out

I'm considering taking up swearing. I figure if I throw around a few bad words, I might get put in a time-out. If the rule is one minute for each year based on age, I could be alone in silence on my bed for over thirty minutes.

If that doesn't work, I could always start speeding around in my car in front of police officers. Acquiring a speeding ticket would result in having to attend traffic school. Eight hours away with a full hour for lunch is awfully tempting. An added plus would be all of the backseat driving I could accomplish after learning some valuable, new traffic laws.

One day, my mother-in-law put a whole new twist on the idea of time-outs after spending the afternoon with three of her grandchildren. While driving home, a speeding car cut in front of her, and after having to brake suddenly, she reacted with a "You idiot!"

The three little angels were flabbergasted at the vulgarity pouring out of their nana's mouth. In unison they blurted out, "Nana, that is a time-out. You said a bad word!"

When she arrived home, she diligently reminded them of the incident and the fact that she deserved a sufficient time-out for her potty mouth. They agreed to fifteen minutes (although she deserved many more based on her age), and off she went with a book in her hand to execute her punishment.

Although they took her book away, her fifteen minutes in silence was refreshing.

Having time alone is a luxury; however, not spending time alone is ludicrous. Moms need moments alone. We devote so much of our time to helping others that we often forget to take care of ourselves. When this happens, we are doing a disservice to our family and to ourselves. This rejuvenation is vital to our well-being — and let's face facts, it feels great! Here are a few suggestions:

- Allow yourself a "girls' night out."
- Grab your favorite magazine and cozy up on the couch.
- Finish that photo album you've been dying to complete.
- Make yourself a bowl of ice cream and window-shop online.

- Take a nighttime shower with the lights out and candles glowing.
- Listen to a radio talk show.

Some of you are early risers by choice. More power to you! Mornings can be serene for me, as long as there is a pot of coffee within reach. There are many ways to make these things happen, even if you don't have a babysitter at your fingertips. Putting the children to bed early one night can do wonders.

This is much easier if you take them to the park at 2:00 p.m. and make them run laps for two hours without stopping. Follow this with a plate of pasta and turkey, and they'll be asleep before the sun goes down.

I love being able to get outdoors too. Even if I have to put the boys in the stroller, the fresh air has a calming effect. You can be as creative as you wish. Just be sure to make alone time happen.

Jesus is a great model of someone who understood the need to have some alone time. The Bible tells us, "Very early in the morning, while it was still dark, Jesus got up, left the house and went off to a solitary place" (Mark 1:35). Mark 6:32 reads, "[Jesus' apostles] left by boat for a quieter spot" (NLT). Are you getting it? Good. Now go!

"Come to me, all you who are weary and burdened, and I will give you rest."

Matthew 11:28

purse paranoia

Whether I'm sitting at a restaurant or attending an event where a chair is involved, I find myself constantly groping at my feet and at the sides of the chair in order to ascertain the location of my purse. One solution for my anxiety would be to wear my purse around my neck like a necklace; the downside would be irreparable damage to my neck caused by the sheer weight of my purse.

Only once was my purse actually stolen, but as a result of that experience, I suffer from an extreme case of purse paranoia. However, my fear relates only to my purse, which hints at the fact that my sickness is self-generated and nonclinical.

The catalyst for my purse paranoia happened when

I accidentally left my purse on the plane after landing at Chicago's O'Hare Airport. When I discovered that I was purseless, I left my two children in my mom's care and ran back to the gate. The agent let me reboard the plane, but, alas, those who were cleaning the plane claimed that they hadn't seen a purse under the seats of the plane.

Sure they didn't.

Alongside the obvious casualty of money and ATM card stood a list of possessions that had taken years to accumulate and would take months to replace. Among those was my California driver's license. Having no driver's license or any other evidence verifying that I was who I said I was, the task of getting on our plane for the last leg of our journey to California seemed impossible.

In the great world of ticket agents and airport security, I was nobody, faceless and unrecognizable, and my two small children were deemed unreliable to vouch for my identity. Thankfully, after many prayers, the powers that be decided that a mother and grandmother traveling with two young children posed no immediate threat to national security and allowed us to board the plane headed for California. We were carefully watched.

Things become lost, stolen, misplaced, or displaced. Some simply vanish. When that happens, we fervently search for those items that hold value and worth to us. In the parable of the lost coin, Jesus tells a story that illustrates the feeling associated with losing something and then finding it. A woman loses a coin and does everything in her power to find it. She lights a lamp and searches and searches until she finally finds the coin. Thoroughly relieved and filled with joy, she calls her friends and tells them of her success in finding the precious coin.

In another parable, a shepherd loses one of his sheep, and even though he has ninety-nine sheep present and accounted for, he goes to the depths of the valley in order to find the one sheep that is lost. When he finds the lost sheep, he calls all of his friends to tell them of his discovery.

Souls get lost also. Satan's goal is to get us lost by diverting our thoughts away from God. He uses friends, fatigue, wealth, accomplishments, exercise, pride, status, self-indulgence, selfish desires, work, busyness, children's sports activities, and other distractions to get us lost. Satan wants to find us far away from God, spiritually empty, and vulnerable. Satan delights when our desire to meet daily with God vanishes.

However, God is always watching and waiting. The instant God senses that we are slipping away, he lights his lamp and begins his search. He taps on our soul, strokes our hearts, thwarts our distant thoughts, and gently tugs us back into his loving arms. God knows that at times we don't want to be found, yet he never gives up his search for us.

Even though my purse was never found, the heaviness of the loss eventually lifted and the contents were finally replaced. My ten dollar sunglasses would have to suffice as a substitute for the more expensive variety, and I'd have to wait until the next round of birthday gift cards and money before I was able to spurge on something more than a plastic purse embellished with painted buckles.

My driver's license photo had to be retaken, and I'm happy to report that in this photo, my hair highlights are visible and clear and the puffy bangs from the nineties have disappeared. That is the good news.

> *"There will be more rejoicing in heaven over one sinner who repents than over ninety-nine righteous persons who do not need to repent."*
>
> *Luke 15:7*

a rare collection

I am collection-challenged. I collect nothing. When I was younger, I saved pictures of Elton John from *Teen Beat* magazine and Snoopy memorabilia, but since then I've become a world-class tosser: everything has a maximum six-month shelf life.

On the other hand, my husband saves everything, including the front pages of major news events from the past twenty years. Among those, we also have the front page from the day each of our children was born, a noble collection indeed. He thinks our kids might need them someday as a resource for writing one of their history reports.

Evidently the World Wide Web with its billions of sites does not hold a candle to the information provided by the local reporters in Southern California.

Admittedly, I've been tempted to discard these pages during our semiannual garage cleanathon. However, I have squelched the temptation, since I do not want to end up with new chip clips or a wrench on Mother's Day.

My oldest child is the queen of collection. Her bedroom currently houses some one hundred or so *Tursiops truncatus*. This is a foo-foo word for bottlenose dolphin. She uses no discretion in selecting dolphin memorabilia for her castle — she has rubber, glass, plastic, wooden, squeaking, chiming, stuffed, photographed, and silk-screened dolphins scattered within the four walls of her bedroom.

Also, she is meticulous about keeping them dusted and placed in just the right places. Any disturbance in the orderly arrangement of her collection sends her into a panic frenzy. My urge to purge the pencil-drawn dolphin families and handmade gifts is often overwhelming, but I sit on my hands and resist. There will be plenty of time for clearing when she is away at summer camp.

God must have an amazing collection in heaven. I picture a room a mile long, yet somehow small and intimate in his eyes. On its shelves are gleaming crystal vases containing broken spirits, each one individually labeled and loved. Above these are photos of the lowly outlined in glistening jeweled frames. Polished golden urns containing withered souls and gently woven baskets carrying hearts laden with loneliness sit side by side.

Among these are elegantly detailed trophies representing

minds that no longer function and brilliant blue velvet boxes embracing the sick, aged, and outcast. An onlooker might see this menagerie as a truly pathetic assortment; however, I visualize God standing there cherishing each and every one of his collected works, lifting each one individually, dusting it off, and placing it back on the mantelpiece next to all of his other trophies and treasures. His entire assortment is of equal value, and each is deliberately cared for as though it is his favorite.

God does not toss out everything that is imperfect, which is a great relief. We are all broken, bandaged, and bruised in some way, whether physically, emotionally, or mentally. However, because of God's unfailing grace, we are not thrown aside. I will probably never become a collector myself. I will leave all of that up to my Father in heaven.

> *"Indeed, the very hairs of your head are all numbered. Don't be afraid; you are worth more than many sparrows."*
>
> *Luke 12:7*

perfectly imperfect!

Perfection is overrated. Since Jesus was the only perfect person, I wonder why I continue to compare myself to others. I suspect my "Mother of the Year" award will forever remain in a vat of melted plastic.

Case in point: I was feeling proud of the fact that I took my baby for his three-month "well-child" just days past his three-month birthday. I sat in the doctor's office reflecting back through my day and my other accomplishments. I took a fun shortcut to school, fed the kids cereal that turned the milk a cool blue color (not to mention had a fourteen-year shelf life), and presented my husband a bowl of cereal with the ideal amount of almonds and dried cranberries.

After the typical height and weight calibrations, the doctor emerged with the customary chitchat. Between tweaks and twists, he raised an eyebrow and stated, "His eye looks a little goopy. How long has the redness been apparent?" Goop? What goop? He is the *third* child!

We had just returned from a road trip with forty high school students from church, so I assumed the redness had been around for two days. Smiling, I explained about the vacation, teenagers, dirt, motor home, and the whole memory-making experience when he gave me the look — the one that says "and you call yourself a responsible mother?"

He went on to explain that my infant son had pinkeye, which was probably contracted from one of the filth-infested fingers admiring his button nose and silky curls during our family bonding soiree.

After convincing myself that I was still a decent mother, I brushed off my injured self-esteem and remembered a question I had. As my mouth opened and the words formed in my brain, Dr. Inspect-a-Lot blurted out a stinging observation. "Huh, I have never seen an infant with dirty fingernails." That one smarted! My infant was just more adventurous and playful than his lackadaisical counterparts.

As he continued with the examination, I mustered up the courage to ask my question. "Did you notice his belly button? There is a black tinge deep inside. Is something wrong?" After poking around and giving it a gentle tug, he responded with the final blow, "It looks like your classic case of dirt. Try a little baby oil and a cotton swab." Ouch!

With my psyche withered, whipped, and beaten, I left with a pinkeye prescription in hand and the threat of social services watching my every move. I buckled my little guy into his car seat and drove home to immerse him immediately in gobs of soapy water as I contemplated the addition of bleach, ammonia, and iodine.

Later that afternoon, my now sweet-smelling baby and I picked up my two other children from school. I was well on my way to overcoming my demoralizing morning. After greeting my daughter, she wasted no time in telling me that I had forgotten to put a drink in her lunch. My older son chimed in immediately thereafter with "Let's get some milk shakes!" Although I could have used one, he was given the standard "Not today" to which he retorted, "Grandparents don't say no like parents do." With a deep sigh, I buckled the children into their seats.

After I shifted the car into reverse, the baby began to cry. To divert his attention the kids and I started in with the chorus "If you're happy and you know it, clap your hands." He was not. We made our way home, constantly reassuring him that he was OK. Our vigorous attempts to bring happiness failed miserably. The three-mile trip seemed endless, and despite our cheeriness, he continued to wail.

Moments later, as I was changing his diaper, I noticed a dark red and purple mark on his inner thigh where the car seat latch had obviously pinched his tender leg — for the whole drive home! The screeches were legitimate.

Way to go, Mom!

Try as I might to be the woman God intended me to be, inevitably I will say the wrong thing to my husband, hurt someone's feelings, raise my voice — again — and snap at my children for misbehaving. However, I am encouraged by the truth that God does not expect me to be a perfect woman, wife, or mother. We serve a forbearing God who deeply loves us and sees through our mistakes. He gently encourages us through trying situations in order to build our character and learn to trust in him.

My crown on earth may be formed out of a soiled dishrag and rubber bands instead of a jeweled tiara and "Mother of the Year" sash, but heaven awaits me with a crown of jewels placed there by the Savior — and that, my friend, *is* perfect.

Because of the LORD's great love
we are not consumed,
for his compassions never fail.
They are new every morning;
great is your faithfulness.

Lamentations 3:22–23

suiting needs

Breakfast comes early during the school week. After wake-up calls, each child groggily climbs the barstools stationed along the kitchen counter. Even though biscuits and gravy are never served, they sluggishly give their orders as if seated in a down-home country café.

I am not one to stick to typical breakfast fare if their a.m. cravings lean toward lunch or dinner favorites. Sending them to school with something in their stomachs is my only goal, and on some days, nutrition is optional.

Since each of the children arrives with different palate passions, I have served everything from canned spaghetti and meatballs to sliced apples and Cheetos. On occasion their grandpa surprises them with a box of donuts, which supersedes any suggestions I have for the morning menu.

Dinner also brings a collection of cravings. Normally I'm not one to concoct four different meals for four diverse tastes, but at regrettable times, I give them a choice. The short orders begin to fly while the "What do you want for dinner?" question still dangles on my lips. "Nachos! Noodles with butter! Grilled cheese with bacon! Grapes and a hot dog!" they shout out one by one. "Dinner with Dad at a restaurant where they don't serve Jello or pizza!" I shout back, but no one is listening.

This frightful decision to offer a choice goes into the "never do that again" file in my brain but slips out now and again.

Like customers ordering from a menu of daily specials or selecting a snack from a vending machine, some people use this method to choose a religion. After inserting their coins, they enter the appropriate letter-and-number combination and push the button — and those spiritual samplings and religious relishes that adequately fit into their lifestyles tumble from within the glass enclosure. Any belief or faith that suits their particular taste is inevitably the one preferred.

I believe that everything in the Bible is true. If I only believed parts of the Bible, I would be imitating a judge, licking the tip of my finger as I flip through the pages of God's Word, deciding which parts are fact and which are phony. I choose not to accept that responsibility.

I do, however, have the ability to decide how I am going

to live my life — by the Bible's standards or by the world's. Making biblically based choices is a daily struggle. Oftentimes human nature takes over, and I find myself pulled by the world and making excuses for my actions, arguing that they pale in comparison to the misdirection of other people. But there are no shades in God's preference for the way we spend our time here on earth.

Picking through and plucking out parts of God's Word that seem to fit our lifestyles is not what God intended. He manages a kingdom that is biblically based and God breathed. We can live it or leave it, but his words can never be changed. I do hope, though, that they have vending machines in heaven, because I have an affinity for cheese puffs.

> *Every word of God is flawless;*
> *he is a shield to those who take refuge in him.*
> *Do not add to his words,*
> *or he will rebuke you and prove you a liar.*
>
> *Proverbs 30:5–6*

artist demands

The things celebrities demand while they are on tour span the spectrum from nutty to notorious. While Britney Spears humbly requests strawberry Pop-Tarts, Cap' n Crunch, and Froot Loops, Gwen Stefani demands twelve individual-sized iced Fiji waters in her trailer and a cornucopia of organic items. Justin Timberlake reserves the entire floor of certain hotels and insists that all door handles be disinfected every few hours. Mariah Carey is a germ freak also. She requests that a new toilet seat be installed before her arrival, and Christina Aguilera combats viruses with her request that one bottle of Flintstones vitamins with extra vitamin C be available in her dressing room.

I suppose I could conjure up my own list of artist

demands, in the event that I would ever be an artist with demands. Bottled water would be nice, although tap water agrees with me just the same. Freshly cut roses and tube-rose with some stargazer lilies would add to the ambiance of my dressing room, which is actually called a closet. A new toilet seat sounds appealing, but bleach works just as well. I like pistachios and Zone Perfect bars, but I have some at home that I can bring. A full-time nanny would be wonderful, but she would have to know the ins and outs of pre-algebra and how to pitch a baseball.

However, citing these ridiculous demands of stars doesn't eliminate a finger pointing back at each of us. There have been times when my phone rang and I let the machine pick up because the caller was someone I didn't want to talk to — I knew the conversation would have lasted over an hour and would center on her complaints. There also was the time I told my fourth grader I was unable to attend his field trip — I actually could have gone but didn't want to spend three hours with a brood of boisterous adolescents.

As Christians, we are admonished to become more like Jesus. What does that look like? Certainly not the "me first" philosophy of many people today. Jesus was the master of putting others before himself. He ministered to the leper, the widow, and the woman who had been hemorrhaging for ten years. Jesus didn't said, "I'm too busy," or "What's in it for me?" Jesus didn't get mad at his people when they rejected him; instead, the Bible tells us that he wept over Jerusalem (Luke 19:41).

Incumbent on each of us as we strive to become more like Jesus is to put aside the prevailing "me first" idea and become a loving servant. The reality that there is still a lot of work to be done in my life comes to expression in the fact that going on a field trip with fourth graders still sounds unappealing — unless the field trip is to Starbucks!

> *Do nothing out of selfish ambition or vain conceit. Rather, in humility value others above yourselves, not looking to your own interests but each of you to the interests of the others.*
>
> Philippians 2:3 – 4

breaking up with debra

Everything about Debra was beautiful. She had thick, smooth, black hair that draped down her back like a velvet curtain. Her skin tone matched that of a cup of coffee with just a hint of cream. On her huge, dark eyes sat lashes that never ended and only required a single coat of black mascara to accentuate their length. She had a slender frame and wore clothes that clung in all the right places. Her smile was composed of blinding white teeth that lined up in ideal rows. She was the best friend a new girl could have.

I was the new girl on the block, and my brother was the new boy. He had his pick of friends, with approximately five guys around his age living within walking distance. On the other hand, I had Bonnie, who lived next door, and Debra, who lived across the street, three doors down. Bonnie was in ninth grade, Debra was in the seventh grade, and I was in sixth grade. Though Bonnie was friendly, the smaller age difference between Deb and me proved to be a match. While Bonnie was thinking about her theatrical performances and which lip gloss matched her fiery-red hair, Deb and I were writing letters that we decorated with flowers, hearts, and boys' names and then folded into origami shapes.

Having a best girlfriend who liked to do many of the same things I did and who loved so deeply was very cool. We shared clothes, sat at the nearby park eating sunflower seeds and drinking Slurpees, bantered back and forth about the men in our adolescent lives as we sauntered through the mall, and spent summers riding the bus to the beach to tan ourselves silly.

Of course, that was before we realized that all of our baking in the sun would result in our faces needing a year's salary worth of Botox injections and chemical peels — and leatherlike thigh skin that would hang over our kneecaps.

As we grew older and our lives changed, we made a serious effort to remain friends. We became roommates, party pals, and bridesmaids. The words *discretion* and *limits* were not part of her vocabulary. I decided that Christian living wasn't nearly as much fun as doing the things that Debra liked to do. However, as hard as I tried to cling to the crazy lifestyle she was living, I began to realize that I needed to make better moral choices.

Since I was a newly married Christian woman who desired children and a life committed to my husband and family, I had to sever my relationship with Debra because she wasn't the influence I needed in my life. Her words weren't uplifting, encouraging, or supportive. The very things that bonded us together in our adolescence now became the things that caused the chasm in our friendship.

So I stopped calling her, and eventually she stopped wondering why so much time had passed between our conversations. As a result of my decision, my marriage became stronger, while hers weakened and then fell apart. I haven't seen or spoken to her in many years.

As I began to seek out new friends, I knew that those friendships needed to be with women who shared the same faith and love for God that I had. Also, the women whom I sought for advice and those with whom I would spend time needed to be walking with the Lord and be morally on the same page as I was. These women needed to respect their spouses and marriage.

Therefore, I made a concentrated effort to cultivate such friends. Although I still have non-Christian friends, there is an intimacy I have with my Christian friends that is missing in my relationships with my non-Christian friends.

Letting go of unhealthy relationships is no simple task. Only God's strength and the faith that he will fill our lives with deep, significant bonds allow us to forge forward with new friendships. Just because we've been friends with someone forever doesn't automatically make them the best friend for us. Some of the greatest women in my life are those I've known for only a few years.

Though time can test a friendship, make time for those who don't test your morals. And a word of advice: Always make sure they wear the same size clothes and shoes you wear. This way your wardrobe will double instantly.

Do not be yoked together with unbelievers. For what do righteousness and wickedness have in common? Or what fellowship can light have with darkness?

2 Corinthians 6:14

girls' night out

About every six weeks during the school year, I get together with a group of friends for a night out. The only requirement for the choice of restaurant is that the food be greasy and the drinks cold. One September night, in lieu of our usual restaurant outing, we decided to attend a baseball game. Now all I had to do was shower and appear somewhat presentable. I wasn't asking for miracles.

My expectations for an uneventful time of getting ready with little interference from my children were naive to say the least. The friendly boys and girls who occupied my home only minutes prior left the building and were replaced with horrific, disregarding, argumentative children the minute I disrobed in anticipation of an uninterrupted shower.

spilt milk

Before I made my way into the shower — and wrapped in a towel — I stopped at the computer in my bedroom to send out a quick email. My one-year-old started pulling at the mouse pad and in no time at all bit a hole right through the middle. After a round of arguing with my daughter over homework, I finally made my way to the shower, although I was followed right up to the door.

As I showered, my youngest grabbed a glass bottle of nail polish from the drawer and began banging it on the glass door of the shower. My scolding echoed off the tile and created an eardrum-shattering noise. When the reverberating sounds ended, I heard an "Ow!" echoing down the hall from the living room. I ignored the screaming. This was no time to start disciplining; it was T-minus 31 minutes.

Upon my earlier than anticipated exit from the shower, my youngest continued his annoying behavior by touching and poking me in places that I did not appreciate being touched. While clutching his hands together, I moved him toward the door of the bathroom. He laughed. I found no humor in the events he found to be hysterical.

When I leaned over to tell him that I was unhappy with his actions, he reached up for a final grope. I straightened up, scooped him in my arms, stared into the mirror, and shouted, "Why, God, can I not have thirty minutes to take a shower and get myself ready without being tormented by a one-year-old?" At that moment, the baby turned and blew a wet raspberry on my cheek. After taking one last look at my sorry self in the mirror, I noticed a large green booger on my shirt. I cried when I got into my car.

I was mad. I couldn't understand why God wouldn't allow me just a few uninterrupted minutes to take a shower and to do something with my hair. Why did I have to fight with my daughter over homework on the second day of school? Why didn't I have a more independent baby who could sit with his brothers and play with cars somewhere far away? Why couldn't my husband get home an hour sooner and whisk everyone off somewhere even farther away? Why tonight?

I know that God can handle my anger. He does not hold my immaturity against me and bring it up again when I am weak and vulnerable. He knows my heart and assures me through his Word that our relationship is much stronger than a few shouts in front of the bathroom mirror. He loves me even though I yell at him every now and then.

My first priority for the evening was to indulge in a plateful of nachos and a bowl of chocolate chip ice cream to numb the experiences of the previous hour. Eventually I forgot about my exasperating exit, and I was able to relax while cheering for our team.

Regretfully, "Shout to the Lord" took on a new meaning that evening, but Jesus forgives and Girls' Night Out remains — and for that I am thankful.

> But you, Lord, are a compassionate and gracious God,
> slow to anger, abounding in love and faithfulness.
>
> Psalm 86:15

pet couture

My neighbor was denied the adoption of a dog. He was disqualified and deemed unfit for dog ownership, not because he saddles up large breed dogs and solicits them as miniature ponies for toddler birthday parties or thinks that cats' feet make reliable good luck charms, but because he answered "No" to the following question: Would the dog be allowed inside your home?

Mind you, he was adopting a dog from a shelter where the average life span for an animal is forty-eight hours, and he lives in Southern California, where the temperature dips to a skin-chilling 55 degrees in the dead of winter.

Also, God just so happened to supply dogs with a brilliantly useful item called a coat of fur.

The days of dogs wearing nylon collars and eating food from mutilated pie tins have been replaced by $500 pet mansions and $120 Swarovski crystal-embedded collars. Pets no longer weather the storms with a simple layer of fur. They are clothed in raincoats and wool sweaters. We no longer take dogs for walks; instead we push them around in strollers or cart them about in $1,500 Louis Vuitton carriers.

My dog, Truman, remains outdoors much of the day and eats and drinks from plastic bowls. From his dingy collar hang rusty tags, and he prefers the cool dirt beneath our pine tree to a $500 doggie mansion. He has lived for fifteen years, glitz free, and has survived without any known complaints. And on any given day, you can still find him sticking his nose beyond the open window of our car, soaking up the smells that surround him while oblivious to the fact that many of his counterparts are sitting in $120 faux lambs wool booster seats.

Perhaps you don't find yourself spending loads of money on frivolous pet supplies or treating your dog better than your own child, but we can all attest to the fact that when we see certain items in the store, we become weak. Like well-trained terriers, we reach into our purses and remove our wallets to make a purchase.

Much of what we purchase we do not need. Much of what we pack into boxes that fill our attics and garages we do not need. Much of what we want we do not need.

spilt milk

Much of what our neighbors have we do not need. Much of what crowds our closets we do not need. Much of what protrudes from our pantries we do not need. We want much; we need little.

God provides exactly what we need, and we choose what to do with what he supplies. The Israelites grumbled when God only provided manna and quail to satisfy their appetites for forty years. As a result, they wished to return to slavery, to lives filled with anguish and trial — but with meat and potatoes frequently on the menu. God kept their tummies full, yet they appreciated nothing. Their whining was relentless.

Instead of being whiners, let's appreciate God's goodness, his provisions, and his unflinching love.

As for dog adoptions, unless you live in Nome, Alaska, and own a hairless dog, the outdoors will serve any dog just fine — even without his $25 all-weather dog shoes.

"Store up for yourselves treasures in heaven, where moth and rust do not destroy, and where thieves do not break in and steal. For where your treasure is, there your heart will be also."

Matthew 6:20–21

battle with the bulging

I hate water balloons. When filling them up with water, I have to leave enough air and space near the neck of the balloon so that the water does not burst out in a dramatic fountain and drench my chest. Also, I dread trying to twist the skinny latex top into a knot without the contents spilling out, leaving the impression that I had a tumultuous tussle with the garden hose.

I don't like being pelted with water balloons either. Since I am a pain pansy who prefers warm to cold water, mixing pain and cold water in a destructive concoction should be avoided. I "sideline participate" in any and all water balloon fights. You will never find me engaging in any paintball wars either. Infliction of pain events never find themselves filling in the blank spots on my entertainment calendar.

On the other hand, kids love water balloons. The peak of my summer vacation as an awkward, long-legged sixth grader was camp. The high point of the week, besides drooling over the hot male teenage counselors, was the water balloon fight. Galvanized steel buckets were placed around the center of the campsite, and each was loaded with a rainbow of bulging latex. At the finish of the official countdown, everyone would grab as many balloons as their hands could hold and heave them at their opponents.

I had my eye on attacking a blond, curly-haired staff member with the biggest balloon I could find. Just as he was sneaking behind someone to pummel them with a blast of cold water, I secretly approached him from behind, risking being discovered at each step. Grabbing the wobbly contents, I lifted my arms into the air and slapped the contents behind his bare neck so that the water soaked both the front and back of his shirt. What transpired in the next seven seconds shocked all in view. Just as I was about to punch the air in celebration, he collapsed. He fell to the wooden deck unconscious, and I fell to my knees, ready to provide mouth-to-mouth resuscitation at the first invitation.

I'm generous.

In a flash I pictured myself in an orange jumpsuit with white slip-on shoes, begging the judge to sentence me to modern-day stoning with water balloons instead of rocks or a flogging with some colorful long balloons used for making cleverly twisted creatures. To my relief, some smelling salts aroused him to consciousness, and my imagined jail time evaporated.

However, there was no hiding from the guilt of having injured an innocent man. Even if I ran as fast as I could, I was severely outnumbered. In addition, the surrounding forest was full of malnourished critters craving skinny adolescents.

Instead of running, I cried with remorse and was quickly forgiven.

God is keenly aware of our sinful nature, and thankfully he doesn't treat us as our sins deserve. He knows we will mess up repeatedly, but he willingly forgives when we sincerely ask for forgiveness. His grace and mercy abound.

I never returned to camp, but I heard that the water balloon brawl was replaced with an egg toss. I hope the counselors were wearing knee pads and helmets.

If we confess our sins, he is faithful and just and will forgive us our sins and purify us from all unrighteousness.

1 John 1:9

dear john

During my freshman year in college, I was famous for twelve seconds. If you blinked or your attention was diverted by an unexpected noise, you would have missed my moment. Thankfully, cameras were readily available, and even though they were the type that required film and were partial to dark room exposure, they captured moments.

At the peak of leg warmers and rushing home to watch the latest episode of General Hospital stood a newcomer named John Stamos. He had jet-black hair feathered in all the right places, wore tight Jordache jeans, and had an amazing way of swooning every eighteen-year-old within ten feet of their televisions. He was yummier than a freshly baked chocolate chip cookie covered in mounds of ice cream and fudge — he was a celebrity.

When word got out that John Stamos would be attending a fund-raiser at our college (at which I and the other girls on our cheer squad would be performing), our screams were louder than a nursery filled with famished newborns.

On the day of the event, the pleats of our skirts hardly moved when we walked, and our faces were accentuated with an ideal combination platter of mascara, eye shadow, and pink blush. I don't remember much about the agonizing game of donkey basketball that pitted the celebrities against the cheerleaders while we all rode on the backs of jackasses and tried to put a basketball into hoops.

However, I do remember the moment when I was famous for twelve seconds. I remember that's how long it took for my friend to take a picture of John Stamos and me locked in an ever-loving embrace and leaning against his limousine. I hoped that the blinding camera flash would result in one clear memory-making photo. What a photo it was!

The black-and-white, glossy, 8 x 10 sat in the rafters of my garage for twenty-five years, untouched, until recently. One day while rummaging through a cardboard box of memories, I happened upon the photo, smiled, and brought it into the house, well aware that it was blogworthy, a must-share-with-others photo.

Since John Stamos has been blessed with a stable

career in television, when I showed the picture to my children, they recognized him immediately. Even my nephew, while checking out the photo on my blog, commented, "Is that Aunt Linda with Uncle Jesse?"

Obviously, reruns of *Full House* are in their repertoire of must-see TV.

I took a digital picture of the photo, posted it on my blog, and mentioned to my readers that I would love to have John Stamos sign his name across the front, knowing full well that (1) John Stamos would never read my blog, and (2) no one who knows John Stamos would ever read my blog.

Five days later, a comment was delivered to my email address. Shock of all shocks, John's mother, Loretta, read my blog! Not only did she read my blog, but she also forwarded the post to John, who in turn arranged for his friend to email me and set up a way to get the photo to him for a signature. A few weeks later, I received the signed photo and an updated head shot was included per my selfish request. "Long time no see. Love and Peace, John Stamos" was scrawled across my photo. He's so clever!

John and I do not spend time arranging double dates, and he never shows up unexpectedly to my boys' Little League games or my daughter's school play. We do not send each other Christmas cards or exchange favorite restaurant ideas. Yet, in a vague, removed, and distant way, he knows who I am, and I was famous for knowing him for an estimated twelve seconds of my life. I have a photo as proof. I should call *People* magazine. They need to know.

People often view God as one who is constantly checking up on his children and who demands perfect behavior while pointing his sizzling staff at all of our mistakes. He is often seen as an Almighty Being ready to fuel every fiery trial that comes our way, hoping to grow our character by testing the direction of our moral compass.

In reality, God is about the moments. He delights in surprising us — in the times we least suspect it — with moments of joy, moments of wow, and moments of random miracles. He loves when we smile, when we laugh, and when we realize that he is the creator of special, unexpected moments.

> *For you make me glad by your deeds, LORD;*
> *I sing for joy at what your hands have done.*
>
> *Psalm 92:4*

easing pain

Ailments arrive hourly at our house. At any given moment a headache, bellyache, backache, side ache, toothache, or earache can appear out of thin air. Delivered regularly, seemingly by UPS, are canker sores, cold sores, sore throats, scrapes, bruises, breaks, and their likenesses. In addition, there are the stuffy noses, colds, flus, itchy skins, bug bites, blisters, and hangnails. However, the level of pain tolerance varies from child to child.

If I were a perfectly gowned and coiffed hostess handing out this year's "Lack of Pain Tolerance" award, the first place sash and tiara would have to go to my daughter. Her motto is "Drama — everyone needs some in their lives." She screams "Ouch!" after having a crumpled, dry paper towel thrown in her direction, and I often have trouble spotting the scrape, bruise, or cut that she claims is distracting her slumber.

Our oldest boy is first runner-up. He receives no scholarship money or bouquet of flowers, since his cries are 50 percent self-induced. After teasing his younger brother to the point of explosion, he generally screams after receiving a well-deserved sock in the arm. But he does get "Best in Show" due to four broken bones and a tonsillectomy all before age eight.

Our middle boy visited the ER for a quick chin stitch. FYI — when you mix soap, running water, and tile with jumping, the result is a half-inch scar across the bottom of your chin. The tears came in patches like a sporadic drizzle, but he admitted that the shot and sewing didn't hurt a bit. The big tears came when the neighbor boy dragged him bareback across the lawn — now that was legitimate tear shedding.

Our youngest has enough bruises on his shins to play a game of "Connect the Dots" due to his insatiable appetite for adventure. He seems to be the one with the highest level of pain tolerance. After he cries for a minute, he shakes off the pain and continues imitating a mountain climber as he scales our cinder block wall.

Pain tolerance and suffering took on a whole new meaning for me after I viewed a movie that depicted the last twelve hours in Jesus' life. I wept uncontrollably. I have read and heard details of the crucifixion and suffering of our Lord Jesus Christ; however, experiencing it visually brought me to my knees. My emotions were palpable.

While watching the suffering of Jesus, I wondered how Mary could watch the unfolding of the events without immediately dying of a broken heart. As a mother, I wept for her and what she had to witness. As a sinner, I cried — knowing that Jesus had suffered for me.

Jesus' pain could never be eased with any form of syrup or salve. His pain eased only after his life ended, but he knew how many lives would be saved through his suffering and death, and, thankfully, this story has a spectacular ending. His burial in a well-guarded tomb is not the end of the story.

After a violent earthquake, an angel of the Lord, who looked like lightning and was adorned in white, sat on top of the rolled-away stone. Some freaked-out guards turned white and shook like rattles. Two women appeared, looking for Jesus, and gasped when they saw the angel. He said, "Do not be afraid, for I know that you are looking for Jesus, who was crucified. He is not here; he has risen, just as he said" (Matthew 28:5–6).

One day we all will meet Jesus face-to-face, touch the nail-pierced hands, and be lovingly held in arms once stretched out on the cross so that we could live eternally in heaven — where we will never have to restock bandages, aspirin, or ice packs.

But God demonstrates his own love for us in this:
While we were still sinners, Christ died for us.

Romans 5:8

hardly an affair

I have three boyfriends. My husband is acutely aware of my attractions and goes so far as to announce their arrival when I happen to be standing outside of viewing distance of the television. They are all fictional, which is why my husband allows their existence. One is a doctor, another is a college student, and the third is a dinosaur.

Dr. Robert Chase is a hospitable young man with stunning wisdom in the medical field. He is tall, blond, and thirty-something, but his brain is what attracts me the most, really. He works for a tenacious doorknob of a human named Dr. Gregory House, yet he continuously remains focused and persistent in healing the acutely ill. Bless his heart.

Ben Covington attends New York University. He is

younger than I am by only a few hundred years. He is the bad-boy type with whom every girl hates to fall in love. You expect the best from his charm and demeanor, yet he continues to cheat on you with a girl named Felicity, is never on time, and has an irresistible way of forgetting his wallet whenever you are together at a restaurant. Although Ben is just short of failing school because of his insatiable drinking habit, he is a fantastic swimmer. He is extremely easy on the eyes, but I like his passion for swimming, really. Swimming is good.

The dinosaur I am proud to call my boyfriend is purple, fun, and lovable. We do not IM much or send text messages because his hands are too big for the small buttons. Although he has been inside our house many times, we have never spoken to each other. He has an uncanny ability to entertain my youngest child for more than seven seconds, and for that reason alone, I love him and he loves me.

I am easily pleased.

All kidding aside, I realize that emotional connections with men other than your husband are no laughing matter. With the increase in technology and the ability to communicate in various ways, "emotional affairs" are on the rise. Since there is no physical contact in these affairs, most regard them as harmless. However, they are extremely destructive to any marriage.

One of the best ways to affair-proof a marriage is to

keep the communication between husband and wife open and honest. Slurring your words to one another prior to falling into a deep slumber does not constitute communication. For many of us, intimate, deep communication needs to be scheduled. Our best conversations often take place in a corner booth while eating a Caesar salad, juicy steak, and buttery side dish — or in any other setting where dinner isn't transported in a paper bag. During these times, honest dialogue allows frustrations to be released rather than left to fester and boil until all communication is destroyed.

Equally important is the physical aspect of communication. Men love to be touched, and they enjoy the feeling they get when their wives hold their hands or walk arm in arm with them. Any simple act of touching lets our partner know that he is important. Even though our touch tanks may be tapped out after being around children all day, our husbands still deserve some of what we have left.

I am sure that marriage demolition could have been avoided if King David and his wife, Michal, would have engaged in some bagels-and-lox pillow talk. The Bible doesn't go into much detail about their relationship, but the glimpse we do have sheds light on why King David couldn't keep his paws off Bathsheba.

After a lengthy absence, David was returning the ark of the covenant to Jerusalem. As the ark entered the city, the people of Jerusalem lined the streets, shouting and singing with joy and worship. David, without a thought, took off his royal robe and, wearing only his undergarments, danced in the streets in demonstration of his passionate love for the Lord. This undignified public display didn't set well with his wife, Michal, who watched from a nearby window.

As soon as she could get him alone, Michal began to berate him by describing his worshipful act as "vulgar" (2 Samuel 6:20). Not surprisingly, King David defended his actions with a lengthy diatribe telling her that the Lord chose him over her father and that he will continue to worship the Lord as he chooses. With that said, he no doubt slammed the door as he left the room. She probably threw all of his clothes out the window, burned his favorite chair, and on his hand-painted portrait blacked out the teeth with permanent marker and gave him a face full of zits.

All hope for meaningful dialogue was now lost. As a result, the Bible relates that she had no children, intimating that the libido was long gone. Emotionally and physically detached from Michal, David fed his desire to be with Bathsheba, which eventually led to the murder of Bathsheba's husband and the death of David and Bathsheba's child. Not exactly harmless.

As for me, I've already given up on Dr. Chase and Ben. They can't seem to return my phone calls with those fictional fingers of theirs. The dinosaur, though, is here to stay. But if Bob the Builder or Diego happens to come along to offer some uninterrupted entertainment for my children, I may ask the dinosaur to return the key to my house. I can be fickle.

Marriage should be honored by all, and the marriage bed kept pure, for God will judge the adulterer and all the sexually immoral.

Hebrews 13:4

write me up

I am sometimes a rule breaker or, better to say, a rule ignorer. I choose to ignore certain rules not out of defiance but out of necessity.

Although I am acutely aware of the sign at the entrance to the theater that reads, "No outside food or drinks," I still stuff my purse with cans of soda to the point where permanent shoulder strap indentations remain. The necessity part comes into play when I realize that I would have to go back to work full-time and find my husband a second job if I purchased popcorn and drinks from the concession stand every time I took our four children to the movies.

I assuage my conscience by buying a tub of popcorn at full price.

Another rule I always break involves taking a shower. Now there are no laws against cleanliness that I know of. In fact, I love taking a shower — just not before I take a dip in the pool. There is a sign outside the community pool that reads, "Please shower before entering the pool." I am not quite sure what I am removing from my body or the bodies of my children by showering before entering a toddler-infested pool where urine, saliva, and mucus run amuck. Isn't that why they use chlorine?

Even though I may turn a blind eye to a rule now and again, I do follow laws, mostly. There are times when I've traversed an intersection on a very yellow light or jay-walked, but I've never brandished a weapon inside a fast-food restaurant or run naked through a mall. I have limits.

Since God created us and knows we need guidance and boundaries, he instituted government-enforced laws recorded in the Old Testament — the famous Ten Commandments as well as laws about sacrifices, celebrations, armed forces, sexual relations, social interactions, and appropriate food — that regulated all facets of life. People assumed all they had to do was follow the laws, and their lives would be deemed holy. Not a bad gig.

At the time Jesus came on the scene, the laws were still in effect, but Jesus placed a new twist on God's intentions. He set ground rules for holy living that were laced with spiritual truth and love. Jesus pulled out the big guns — teaching us how to practice self-control, be patient and kind, love an irritating neighbor, adopt a nonjudgmental attitude, have compassion on an adulteress, rub cheeks with a tax collector, sip coffee with an enemy, become self-sacrificing, and embrace a leper. Some people were amazed and frustrated, while others were changed.

I judge too often. I find fault in others. I hate taxes. I am curt with slow cashiers. I am often selfish. However, God's love runs deep, and his grace sustains me. I am a Jesus-follower, yet I still break rules and an occasional law because I am a work in progress. One day I will be like Jesus — just not this side of eternity.

Oh, by the way, I'm working on the soda in the purse thing.

The law of the LORD is perfect,
  refreshing the soul.
The statutes of the LORD are trustworthy,
  making wise the simple.

                        Psalm 19:7

coming clean

After fifteen months of marriage, I became divorced. I had failed miserably at making a good decision, thinking I knew what was best for me. Since then, I've become keenly aware that God knew best the type of man I needed in my life. While driving to the church office and acknowledging this fact, I told the Lord I was giving up control in choosing a mate.

I pulled into the church office parking lot, trekked up the stairs, and asked about the location of the lost and found. My Bible was MIA. In a split second, as I searched through the pile of misplaced Bibles, I decided I wanted to volunteer for one of the ministries at my church. I inquired about high school ministry so I could experience for a second time teenage angst and narcissism, for which I was well trained and highly qualified. The woman at the reception area was appreciative that I was willing to serve in this ministry and gave me contact information.

After making the necessary contacts, I was about to embark on my first official Sunday as a volunteer in the high school department. As I entered the room, I was greeted warmly by a well-dressed guy with nice muscles and a captivating personality. As we shook hands, a voice in my head said, "You are going to marry this guy." Shrugging off my subliminal voice as a caffeine malfunction, I explained that this was my first morning as a high school volunteer, after which he graciously offered a grand tour of the department. Eight months later, we were engaged!

As we began to date and share our life experiences, I had to make a decision. I was either going to share only the parts of my life that were clean and happy, or I'd dump the whole garbage can over his head and then see if he still thought I was worth his effort after he wiped away the muddle. I selected the latter because I knew that God had his hand in our relationship — and since he did, honesty was necessary.

In choosing this path, I risked rejection, but I loved this man and did not want our relationship to have secrets hidden in caves of deceit. Consequently, after a few dates I revealed that I had been divorced and that in college I had dabbled in things I should have stayed away from. These admissions didn't make him cringe or run away. He had his stories, and I had mine. In spite of these seeming obstacles and because of our mutual honesty, we were married seven months later.

Our sixteen years together have had their share of heartache and praise, yet I am confident that nothing can change the fact that my husband loves me. On some occasions he may not like me, but he will always love me.

In the same way, our past and the mistakes we have made do not cause God to love us any less. He sees everything and loves us in spite of our bad decisions. His love is limitless. His grace is a lasting gift. His mercy endures for eternity. His arms are always open. He continually welcomes us home. He holds us close to his heart and never lets us go. He forgives. He erases our mistakes. He is forever awesome!

I am convinced that neither death nor life, neither angels nor demons, neither the present nor the future, nor any powers, neither height nor depth, nor anything else in all creation, will be able to separate us from the love of God that is in Christ Jesus our Lord.

Romans 8:38–39

please don't talk

Yolanda Yak-a-Thon lives in one of the rooms in our house. Yolanda is a walking wealth of information. Her subject matter ranges from repeating the dialogue of the last television show she watched to waxing eloquently about the life span of a honeybee. Give her a minute, and she will tell you what is going to take place in her life for the next six months or what has taken place the previous twelve.

Yolanda loves to share.

Oral book reports, poetry recitals, and giving answers to questions are her specialty. In her dreams, heaven has golden streets lined with stages, microphones, and huge audiences craving her words.

Charlie Chatter also resides in our house. His jabber

generally consists of sharing scenes from the playground, facts about the brain, and corny jokes. When Charlie is overly tired, he begins to create conversation starters. He'll even evoke questions that require more than five minutes of explanation. *Dad, how does a car engine work?* Often we find ourselves playing the "quiet game" with this one.

He never wins.

Peter Prattle has graduated from speech therapy. At one time we prodded words to come out from hiding, and now we cannot stop the momentum of the speeding speech train. "Were God and Jesus here with the dinosaurs?" and "How do trees go to sleep?" are typical questions. I half jokingly suggest he search the Internet for answers instead of seeking answers from me. He is our only child who wants you to join him as he sits on the toilet. He finds complete joy in filling every conversation bubble with more questions, caring little about the surroundings.

Number four is Pat the Parrot. He lacks any original thought. Every word from his mouth is a continuation of conversations started by others or the repeat of former inquiries. This causes an upheaval of "He's copying me!" which is a severe felony in the preschooler book of regulations.

Recently I caught up with my girlfriend as we walked our children to their classrooms. At the moment I arrived by her side, she was swimming in a pool of jabber. As I grinned, in full understanding of her pain, I interrupted with,

spilt milk

"Do you ever get tired of listening?" "Yes!" she retorted, obviously beaten down by babble.

I am truly thankful that my children have a voice and can form words and speak, but I do find myself wishing for a "quiet game" marathon. There are times when I've asked one or more of them to please stop talking so I can think.

However, God never grows tired of listening. In fact, he desires our conversation more than anything. Whether we share casual conversing while doing the dishes or serious requests on bended knees, he loves to hear our voices. God is the perfect listener who never wants to play the "quiet game."

"Then you will call on me and come and pray to me, and I will listen to you."

Jeremiah 29:12

wit's end

Interrupted sleep is one of the most maddening occurrences that can happen to a person, especially when the interruption is utterly unnecessary. Waking every two hours to care for a pain-free, well-fed, and comfortable baby can transform a normally friendly mommy into an angry, half-crazed pit bull. I speak from experience.

My youngest was nearing the nine-month mark and to my dismay was in the habit of waking up every two to three hours for no apparent reason. No warm baths, full tummies, long evening walks, or other old wives' tale remedies forced my baby onto the shores of Sleepyville for the night. Allowing him to cry his way to sleep was out of the question because his room was located right in the area of the other children's bedrooms. The shriek from his cozy crib would surely wake the others, I reasoned, and aside from sleepy boys, a savage, sleep-deprived teenage girl would send all of us to anger therapy.

Each night my husband and I prayed that this would be the night the baby magically slept for more than two hours in a row and caught forty winks rather than seven. However, each night we'd wake up to a crying baby, thinking, "Here we go again." One of us would rock the baby until his peaceful snores rumbled and his body became boneless — that is, until we gently placed him in his crib. Then suddenly, as if a locomotive had jetted through his window, he would sit up, completely alert.

How does a snoring, limp baby suddenly become wide-awake? I have no answer, but I can tell you that muttering under your breath and clinching your teeth does not help, and your teeth hurt afterward.

As weeks passed and I had resorted to using a bleach pen to hide the dark circles under my eyes, God spoke to me through a devotion titled "Help Me." As I read the words and the accompanying Scripture, I realized that instead of getting angry at God, I needed to ask for his help.

Some of us are a little slower than others. Then again, you'd be slow too if you were sleep deprived.

So I prayed, "God, I need your help. Please give me the wisdom I need to get the baby to sleep through the night. Help me, help me, please help me."

The next afternoon, the baby and I visited the doctor for a well-baby appointment. When the pediatrician asked me how everything was going, a flood of tears drenched my face. I told my sleepless-night story and informed him that, given his list of credentials, he must have the magical potion we could give our baby. He came up with an amazingly creative and highly professional answer: "Let him cry."

Now I'm a mother of four children, and I knew that his advice was right on, but what he didn't understand were our living arrangements. If I allowed my baby to cry himself to sleep for the forty-six or so minutes required to accomplish the desired blissful sleep, all of the household occupants, including the dog, were going to suffer.

As we drove home, I pondered the doctor's advice as the baby yawned and we made our way through every traffic light and stop sign. While undoing the car seat and lifting him out, I lectured. "You are tired and going to sleep. I will not be bothered if you cry for three hours, and I will not, unless your room is on fire, come into your room. Do you understand?" The last question was rhetorical — a formality. He cried for twenty-one minutes.

Eventually, he was off to Snoozeland! At this point I wasn't kicking up my heels too high. The clock read noon, and in the evening I had to vault over another hurdle. But I was coming to see that trusting God and continuing to ask for his help were the cornerstones of any success I would have at tough love.

Nighttime rolled around, and I informed my husband of my plan. Our baby was going to Baby Boot Camp, starting that very night. This time I prayed that the rest of the family wouldn't be interrupted by the wails of a baby experiencing his first night in the trenches. He did not give up easily and cried for one hour and thirteen minutes, to be exact. God's blessing through this was that none of the other children woke up. After each night the crying time decreased, and by the third night the baby had slept for ten hours and hadn't shed a single tear.

The next morning I was so well rested and happy that I was ready to hand out money to the kids and serve cotton candy and sodas for breakfast. I'm thankful to God for giving me the ability to heed the advice of a wise doctor and for sustaining me through the training process. God helped me. What a relief!

Sleep is a wonderful thing.

> *"For I am the LORD your God*
> *who takes hold of your right hand*
> *and says to you, Do not fear;*
> *I will help you."*
>
> Isaiah 41:13

boxes

I once unwrapped a beautifully decorated gift, and staring me in the face was a box labeled "Jumper Cables." As I gazed at the picture, wondering what I was going to do with jumper cables, the gift giver blurted out, "Don't let the box fool you."

Generally speaking, boxes are the precursor to what lies within, and the outcome is extremely predictable when the box and the gift match. "Good things come in small packages" is a saying that is associated with velvet-covered boxes. These black and blue beauties are generally home to pricey pieces that belong on your neck, ears, fingers, or wrist. "How beautiful!" and "You shouldn't have!" are normally shouted when the tiny top opens and the splendor is revealed.

spilt milk

Specialty department stores treasure their goods in an array of box colors — silver, gold, or white. Their name is usually printed across the top, which gives the receiver a general clue as to its contents. The handbag you've had your eye on or those jeans that fit just right may be tucked beneath the crispy, white tissue.

Neon pink or pale blue boxes usually hold garments (if you can call them that) with material missing in some significant areas. In my opinion, the designers of these naughty nighties should include directions. I am never certain where the strings go and the lace doesn't, but I do know that if any personal part is covered by material and not exposed, the outfit is on incorrectly.

There are also the quaint, one-of-a-kind boxes that boutiques usually provide their customers. These are sturdy boxes tied with a thick satin ribbon, with a logo often embossed in gold on the top corner. Lifting these box tops may reveal a sweetly scented candle or a picture frame adorned in gems and rhinestones, something handmade, or a rare find at Blooming Expensive department store.

My favorite box is of the pale pink cardboard variety. The long flaps on the sides are anchored with shiny tape, and the front flap is gently tucked. The name of the institution is printed in black across the top, and the insides are perishable. Size doesn't matter in the least. Whatever is in the box is certain to be freshly baked, frosted, layered, drizzled, iced, sprinkled, or whipped. As long as the coconut and cherries are MIA, I'm not picky about the contents!

I realize that loving these boxes more than others places me in the minority, but when my husband walks into the house holding a pink box, my insides get all happy. If at that moment I could blink my eyes and have all the kids be sound asleep in their beds and a pot of coffee brewing in the kitchen, my fantasy would be complete.

The greatest gift of all entered this world and was placed in a wooden box. Bible scholars describe this box as a feeding trough for animals. The first resting place for Jesus, Son of God, King of kings, and Lord of lords, was a hay-lined box, unsuitable at best. He should have been brought in on a golden chariot pulled by valiant white horses; he should have been wrapped in 100 percent European cotton and lying in a velvet-lined cradle. But what I think doesn't matter. We will never understand the mystery behind God's plan. As the Messiah, Jesus was full of miracles and carried with him the promise of eternal life for all who would accept his gift.

The box was irrelevant. The gift that was inside changed the world.

The fact of the matter is that good things come in all types of boxes. Great ones come in mangers.

The wages of sin is death, but the gift of God is eternal life in Christ Jesus our Lord.

Romans 6:23

drumsticks and whale vomit

A woman in Delaware successfully sued a local nightclub after she attempted to avoid a cover charge by climbing into the club through the bathroom window. She fell on the floor and broke two of her teeth. Another woman collected over $100,000 from a restaurant after she slipped on a spilled drink and broke her tailbone. The drink was on the floor because she had thrown the beverage at her boyfriend after an argument.

Lawsuits have run amuck.

Years ago I could have been the winner of a big-bucks lawsuit; however, in the eighties, people were not as litigious as they are today. They took responsibility for their own actions — the audacity! I was standing in a crowded room at age eighteen watching a hot new band called Van Halen erupt onto the stage. The venue was small enough for me to see Mr. Roth's armpit sweat rings on his shirt.

By the third song we were all embroiled in raucous dancing. As the drummer struck his last kaboom, accompanied by a fling of his sweaty hair, one of his drumsticks broke in half, flew through the audience, and struck my forehead, leaving a slight gash.

I wish I could tell you that the blood was oozing from my forehead and dripping down my face, leaving deep, red stripes, but I would be lying. Yes, it bled, but insignificantly. I wish I could tell you that the hot lead singer leaped from the stage, swooped me into his hairy man arms, kissed my boo-boo, and stuffed gobs of money down my shirt to cover medical expenses and mental distress. I wish I could tell you that the security guards asked if I would like a backstage pass and autographed poster of the band. If I told you these things, I would be lying. No one did anything.

After wiping the blood from my forehead, I reached down and picked up the culprit. Smiling, I stuffed the splintered stick into my purse. No one within fifty feet had a souvenir of that caliber!

One man in the Bible who accepted responsibility for his actions ended up as whale vomit, which, as it turned out, wasn't all that bad. God told Jonah to go to a large city called Nineveh and tell all the wicked people to change their ways. This journey would take three days. The blisters from his sandals would be atrocious!

Instead, Jonah boarded a ship and sailed in the opposite direction — as if he could run away from God. Suddenly a storm threatened their ship. Each crew member played rock-paper-scissors to determine whose god was culpable for the calamity. Jonah lost.

At this point Jonah could have denied any blame and cried foul. He was already in the habit of running away. Instead, Jonah took responsibility and convinced the crew to throw him overboard in the hope of forestalling the fury. His idea worked! The sea calmed, and before he drowned, a giant fish swallowed him. He stayed in the fish for three days and three nights, without room service or chocolates on his pillow at night. Couldn't he sue for mental anguish?

As children of God, we are to speak truth, take responsibility for our actions, and avoid placing the blame on others. Sometimes the cost is high, but the reward is a renewed and strengthened relationship with God. That's much better than gobs of money, right?

You were once darkness, but now you are light in the Lord.
Live as children of light (for the fruit of the light consists in
all goodness, righteousness and truth) and find out what
pleases the Lord.

Ephesians 5:8 – 10

walking tasha

On most days her hair is a faint lavender hue — unintentionally. She often wears an array of sweatshirts, some of which have been designed by the painted hands of her grandchildren, yet she has also been seen in her bubblegum pink robe and aqua blue polyester pants. She strolls up and down the sidewalk, deliberately dragging her limp right foot all the way around the block.

The eggshell-colored walls of her home are adorned with a picture of Jesus and a paper photo of President George Bush. A cardboard box on her dining room table holds a handwritten envelope giving explicit directions for donations to be given to Calvary Church and the Republican Party. Her dog regularly escapes her yard and is impossible to corral. This is due in part to the confines of the house from which she rarely emerges.

I haven't been around seniors for any length of time (unless, of course, you count my mother, who, by virtue of her driver's license alone is regarded as a senior — by no means by her looks, attitude, or physical state), but I know that stereotypical seniors are feeble, severely wrinkled, and expert rummy players. However, for this particular senior, small talk was her true passion.

With four active kids around me, mustering up the attention to listen to details about how long the bus took to arrive at our house or the fact that Tasha, her dog, ate a sandwich off the kitchen counter was a last priority, so avoidance was the tactic of choice.

Befriending her was difficult — a time management issue. On the other hand, my daughter was elated when she was offered a dollar for walking Tasha around the block. This chore required daily attendance, along with a listening ear the size of New Hampshire.

My daughter would often return home several minutes after we expected her. When I questioned, "What were you doing?" she simply stated with a grin and a hop in her step, "Talking!" They were a perfect match.

Zacchaeus was a man with very few friends. No one wanted to be around him, let alone listen to what he had to say at any given time. He was a hated tax collector who danced on the financial downfall of others. One day Jesus came to Zacchaeus's town, and a great crowd gathered around Jesus. Since Zacchaeus was height challenged, he climbed a nearby sycamore-fig tree in order to have a bird's-eye view of Jesus and remain sufficiently hidden in the branches of the tree.

Perhaps Zacchaeus felt unworthy to be seen by Jesus. What Zacchaeus didn't know was that Jesus liked him. He even loved him. That's why Zacchaeus was surprised when Jesus, peering through the branches, acknowledged him and asked him to climb down because he was going to visit him at his house.

People were shocked — even disgusted. How could a man like Jesus want to spend time with a man like Zacchaeus? Because Jesus came to save those who are lost (Luke 19:10). Jesus doesn't judge people by their careers. Jesus loves the lonely. Jesus isn't annoyed with mundane conversation. Jesus seeks out the friendless. He hugs the hurting. Jesus would have no problem walking Tasha. He would listen to my neighbor for as long as she was willing to speak. Jesus seeks what I avoid — how humbling!

My daughter doesn't walk Tasha anymore, and my neighbor is no longer found sauntering down the sidewalk. She is leaping in heaven as she walks her dog. Her robe is no longer pink, and her right foot works perfectly well. She talks to everyone she sees, and they are happy to listen — and she sees the face of Jesus in all of his glory every day while they talk and talk and talk.

spilt milk

May the Lord make your love increase and overflow for each other and for everyone else.

1 Thessalonians 3:12

bring on the clowns

I laughed. Not out loud, of course, but close. During a recent church service, our pastor encouraged us to spend the next few weeks making an effort to meet the needs of others. I knew he could not possibly be speaking to me, because as a wife and a mother of four, I meet needs constantly, which often makes me feel like a deflated balloon after a birthday celebration.

I had just returned from a trip to Ohio to visit my brother and his family. In preparation for our five-hour flight, I stuffed the innards of four backpacks with enough craft supplies, puzzles, books, and DVDs to entertain a classroom of thirty students for two straight weeks.

What was the result of my preparation? The batteries

failed on the portable DVD player midway through "There Goes a Fire Truck," and the mini-Play-Doh containers were tossed aside within seconds. The snacks were ignored in favor of airplane fare, and the books were flipped through at Mach speeds. Those few activities killed only the first hour. Desperate to amuse two small boys, I asked the flight attendant if she knew of any clowns aboard the plane with pockets full of balloons, squirting flower rings, magic tricks, and face paint. She smiled and offered me a gin and tonic free of charge.

During our stay in Ohio, I equipped the oldest children in gear appropriate for riding motorcycles. The special pants, shirts, gloves, and boots weren't technically required, but my city kids were intent on replicating an X Games motocross superstar since the equipment was available. When riding vehicles became boring, I flung them across a twenty-foot zip line, which generously left my arms feeling stretched out like an overused bungee cord.

While my husband stayed back to manage our home and keep working, I juggled the responsibility of feeding, napping, and entertaining our four children, in someone else's home. When our youngest woke up in the middle of the night regurgitating on the blankie he cannot live without, I cried. This was no vacation. Although I had sufficient help from my mother and sister-in-law, given all that was required of me, my breakdown was inevitable. At this moment, I was grateful for Mel-O-Creme, a spectacular ice cream stand within walking distance of their home.

Moms meet needs 24/7. Most days I feel beat. As 2:00 p.m. nears, my eyes are heavy, and I feel like taking a short nap on the kitchen rug. But before I can close my eyes, one child wants a snack, another one needs to go poop, and the two oldest want me to play a card game with them. All plans for a quiet nap go up in smoke.

When I seem to be stretched beyond my capacity to endure and feel like I need to be hooked up to an IV of Red Bull, I need to remind myself that I am God's child and that he meets my needs, just as I continue to meet the needs of my children. Unlike me, though, his arms never tire, he never loses patience, and he never needs a nap. I just hope that in heaven I can have soft-serve ice cream piled high in a cup filled with brownie bites.

See what great love the Father has lavished on us, that we should be called children of God! And that is what we are! The reason the world does not know us is that it did not know him.

1 John 3:1

stealing fruit

No one notices when he slips into the house and begins to steal fruit from me. Starting off slowly, with just a small piece, he slithers behind my back and begins to take bigger and bigger slices, all the while letting out deep monsterlike belly laughs as he slinks around the house unseen. That fruit that the enemy is constantly trying to steal is love, joy, peace, patience, kindness, goodness, faithfulness, gentleness, and self-control. The robber's unwelcome influence was never more evident than on one particular October morning.

Since my idea of a nutritious breakfast is not Starburst candy and cheese puffs — as requested that day by my youngest — I issued a firm "No!" He responded by flopping onto the kitchen floor, belly down, screaming and kicking. In his bedroom when I tried to remove his pajamas in order to dress him for the day, he came at me with flailing fists, imitating a young boxer being pulled out of the ring before the end of round two. Tilting my head backward to avoid a good slug, I managed a diaper and jeans but no shirt. Tugging to escape my grip, he ran out of the room screaming as if he was possessed. I then slammed the drawer shut, which made me feel better.

The first slice of fruit was gone.

In round two of "Let's test Mom's patience," my four-year-old changed his outfit four times in thirty minutes, leaving a trail of clothes strewn in his bedroom and down the hall. When I tried to put a diaper on him with the "wrong" picture affixed to the front binding, he screamed incessantly, "I don't want this diaper!" He then proceeded to dirty the fresh "wrong" diaper, ensuing in a change into the "right" diaper. Four-year-old — 1, Mom — 0. Filled with frustration, I threw the soiled diaper across the room, which pelted our sleeping dog, and screamed into my hands in an effort to control all other outbursts that were begging to escape.

Another slice of fruit had disappeared.

Not to be outdone by his younger siblings, my oldest boy fought with me about his clothing choices for the day. A soiled but favorite shirt he had worn for the past two days was his idea of the perfect shirt to wear again. To solidify the logic of his choice, he reasoned that the clean, unstained shirt would inevitably get dirty at school. Then turning his innocent blue eyes in my direction, he added, "I know how you don't like it when I have dirty shirts at school." My eyes narrowed, and in an unfriendly voice, I shouted, "Get dressed!"

More fruit — vanished.

The icing on the proverbial cake was when my oldest yelled at me to quit making her bed. She doesn't like nice favors. To demonstrate her displeasure, she stomped her way to the front door, grunting like a wounded bear. Gathering up her Alaska report from the table, I took one last look at the pages before stuffing it into her backpack. Much to my dismay, I saw that the report was done in pencil — the sheet of instructions I had glanced over earlier clearly stated that students were to use ink. Good-bye fifteen points.

Good-bye more fruit.

Although the clock read 8:30 a.m. and I still had a full day ahead of me, my heart and soul had been emptied. In his sly and slithery way, Satan had snuck into my morning and robbed me of my joy. I was tried and tested, and I had failed completely. Embarrassed, I asked God to restore my character and allow me another chance. Even though my anger was still heavy, as I continued to pray, God slowly massaged my soul to a softened state and brought me back to where I needed to be emotionally.

By midday the morning's meltdowns were a faint memory. My little kids took a two-hour nap while I enjoyed the bottom fourth of a bag of potato chips. I followed the chips with an apple and banana in an attempt to cancel out the fat and grease, but I don't think I was successful. I then ate a large slice of strawberry cake. I was beginning to feel better.

We let the enemy in the door when we fail to maintain a close, intimate relationship with God and instead try to go about our lives solo. Unfortunately for me, fruit of the Spirit does not come in a small pill-like form sold at the local drugstore. This fruit is procured by diving into God's Word, followed by a ton of prayer. The good news is that his food is fat and calorie free. Bring it on!

The fruit of the Spirit is love, joy, peace, patience, kindness, goodness, faithfulness, gentleness and self-control.

Galatians 5:22−23

calamitous cartwheels

With the exception of my eyelashes and belly button, every inch of my being ached. I felt as if I had just climbed Mount Everest, barefooted. These aches and pains were the consequences of a brain warp in which I thought I was in my twenties.

Earlier, I had watched my daughter painstakingly maneuver through unbalanced cartwheels that ended in clumsy thuds. I'd decided she was in desperate need of some instruction.

While my husband watched the scene unfold while trimming roses, he shook his head and grinned with one of those, "You have no idea what you're getting yourself into" smirks. I poised my body like a professional pigtailed gymnast, waited for my daughter's undivided attention, and tumbled through a stunning cartwheel that elicited a "Cool, Mom, teach me!" to erupt from her lips.

If I'd had any sense, I would have ended the exhibition after the first pointed toe.

However, the folly of pride reared its ugly head as my audience of four watched with bated breath. Pushing aside the wimpy cartwheels, I quickly moved onto round-offs. After each barefooted landing and arched-back finish with hands thrown in the air, I wondered to myself, *When did the ground get so hard?*

Following twelve dynamic demonstrations coupled with pauses for mother-daughter coaching, we moved on to the wheelbarrow races. The younger siblings got in on the action, and soon a burst of relay races exploded in our front yard. My daughter continued the cartwheel dance, all the while seeking encouragement, and the baby sat bouncing on his behind, clapping as if he were seated in the front row of a three-ringed circus.

Although the sun began to set, I was not relenting. My "Fun Mom" trophy was waiting for me in the banquet hall, and I was mulling over my acceptance speech. With my husband's "It's getting dark" comment, my bubble burst and reality seeped in. Dinner was hiding out in the refrigerator somewhere, and everyone at once decided they were starving. With the cheers still ringing in my ears, I gathered up the performers and headed indoors.

spilt milk

After dinner, baths, and the kids tucked in bed, I groaned my way to the couch. Following three ibuprofen and several slurps of water, I made a rapid determination that as a mom of four, pregnancy and age have left me acutely less agile. My exquisite executions resulted in a three-day recovery period to regain normalcy and in severe equilibrium failure. All was not lost, however. My daughter soon mastered cartwheels and even taught herself how to do the splits.

No way was I coaching that one!

How refreshing to know that God's strength, power, and wisdom are limitless. When our earthly bodies fail, he carries us. When emotionally we cannot take another step, he brings us strength. When burdened with past sins and failures, he releases our load and leads us toward forgiveness and hope. And when our stresses overrule our thoughts, he brings peace. There is nothing too big for God.

In time, the kids moved on to roller skating, doing loops from the driveway, down the sidewalk, and up the walkway. As I stood watching from the front window, I thought, *Did I ever tell them I was a floor guard . . . at Skate Junction . . . for three years?*

"Honey, have you seen my skates?"

He gives strength to the weary
and increases the power of the weak.

Isaiah 40:29

mission possible

My early attempts at evangelism came at a price. At the age of eight, dressed in a Girl Scout uniform, brown knee-high polyester socks, felt beanie, and green skirt, I enthusiastically asked a neighbor girl if she would like to pray with me to become a Christian. My tenacious desire to get everyone aboard the train bound for heaven came in the wake of a church service that had challenged the fourth grade students to preach the Good News to our unsaved friends and loved ones, lest they be left behind.

What preceded the conversation is unclear; I may have offered her a Ding Dong and lemonade if she repented of her sins and claimed Jesus as her Savior. What I do remember is her jumping up and down the entire time I was guiding her through the prayer of salvation. Although I was sure to keep my eyes tightly closed in order to circumvent derailing any risk of the prayer not working, my keen ears heard her jumping up and down while breathlessly repeating the words I was saying.

Just as I was about to seal her destiny in eternity with a strong "In Jesus' name. Amen," I was rudely interrupted by a warm, wet sensation on my legs. A wandering dog, assuming that my green uniform and brown socks were a tree, proceeded to relieve himself on my legs. The tag on his collar was clearly labeled "Satan."

That event ended my neighborhood evangelism.

Nineteen years later, while volunteering in youth ministry, I was asked to go on a mission trip to Mexicali, Mexico. I was teaching elementary school at the time and happened to have Easter break at the same time the trip was scheduled. This adventure would dispel any thoughts of relaxing at the beach and engaging in long lunches with friends. Even though all self-centered signs for traveling to Mexicali read "NO," begrudgingly I went.

For eight days, I endured hundreds of high school students, overflowing outhouses at the tent camp, miles of dust and dirt, no running water or electricity, long lines for food, days void of soap, and attempts at sleeping in a tent with chatty freshman girls. I asked God if there wasn't another place where I could evangelize. Perhaps the children of Hawaii or those sitting near the shores of Florida needed flannel board stories and cotton ball crafts. Couldn't I just pray for the thousands of people between here and Australia who have a heart for mission work instead of going forth myself?

God ignored my endeavor to remain selfish and brought the mission field to me — when I wasn't looking. Where in the world did I ever get the idea that in order to serve God I had to travel to a Third World country? While delivering preassembled bags of popcorn and juice bags to the eight or so children occupying my backyard, I suddenly realized that my mission field was located right in my neighborhood. Although there are times when I resent having the entire neighborhood in my yard traipsing through the mud, screaming that they stepped in dog poop or leaving popcorn shrapnel and empty juice bags scattered around, I know the kids feel welcome — and that brings me contentment. In some small way I am loving them for Jesus.

For now, the high school age kids live on another street, and the only outhouse is in front of a home under construction. We still have dirt and dust, but this time there is running water and electricity. I even have a place where I can take a warm shower every day, even though I often skip a shower altogether. I live in my mission field, and if God chooses to place me somewhere else, then I will prayerfully go — as long as there are no wandering dogs.

Whether you eat or drink or whatever you do,
do it all for the glory of God.

1 Corinthians 10:31

nothing but the truth

For brutal honesty, second graders score a perfect ten. If you are experimenting with a new hairdo or modeling a trendy outfit, grab a seven-year-old and ask them what they think of "the new you." You will always get a straight-forward answer.

This I know from experience. On my first day of teaching second grade, I was approached by eager and curious boys and girls. As they sat wide-eyed in a semicircle around my feet, I asked if anyone had any questions. In addition to "How old are you?" and "Are we having PE today?" one inquisitive boy asked why part of my front tooth was brown. I didn't realize how brown it actually looked to the keen eye of a meddling seven-year-old, and

I proceeded to inform him that my tooth was stained from years of drinking coffee. If I had given him the complete dissertation of how my chipped front tooth was covered with a cheep veneer that had discolored over time, we would have had an interrogation lasting until Christmas break.

On another day, a student asked why the area above my lip was darker than the rest of my face. Before I could find the nearest burning candle and perform a quick upper-lip hot wax, I smiled and replied, "I tan more above my lip than on the other parts of my face." I confused him enough to squelch any more unbearable questions from leaking out of his despairingly honest lips.

Moments later, I was lifting my arm to wave in a few stragglers from the playground, and a student informed me that I had a hole in the armpit of my sweater and a stain on my pants. The outspokenness was killing me. By this time my self-esteem was dangling somewhere near the bottom of my shoe as my significant flaws continued to be pointed out by up-front preadolescents.

Not unlike my second graders, I consider myself an observant flaw finder. I am a world-class picker, tucker, pointer outer, and fixer. I am the good friend who informs you of a snippet of something wedged in your pearly whites. You've got a tag sticking up from your collar? I am your tucker. If you need the dirt brushed off the left side of your hiney, or your belt has skipped a loop, you can count on me to let you know. And if you stepped on something that needs to be unstuck, I am your puller offer.

Only a select few have this uncanny claim to fame, and I take my job quite seriously. There is nothing worse than smiling in the mirror at your image only to realize that a pepper flake has nestled in your front tooth. Add to the fact that you have just completed a ten-minute conversation with your husband's boss that included lots of teeth showing, and the humiliation is complete. Toothpick, where were you?

Men are not usually the first to fix or tuck, but they do take informing and noticing to a whole new level. Men have no trouble truth telling when one of their friends has gotten fat, received a bad haircut, purchased a stupid T-shirt, or shared an idiotic idea. The recipient of these discouraging disclaimers reacts with laughter and perhaps a slap on the back and certainly never considers these infraction findings a reason to fracture a friendship. On the other hand, men are smart enough to know that a smidgen of these cutting comments to a woman would open up the floodgates of fits and sobs. The words "You look fine" generally have the same reaction.

Shadrach, Meshach, and Abednego were virtuosos of verity. The book of Daniel tells us that King Nebuchadnezzar had a ninety-foot statue built out of gold, probably not in the shape of a fat-bellied yak. He required the people of Babylon to fall down and worship the statue when all kinds of music played. If anyone chose to disobey the command of the king, they would be thrown into a blazing furnace — without marshmallows, chocolate bars, and graham crackers.

Being Jewish and followers of God, Shadrach, Meshach, and Abednego refused to worship anything or anyone other than God. When the king got word of their utter defiance, he was furious and ordered them to tell the truth about defying the king's command. Without hesitation, knowing their fate, they told the king that they would never worship his image of gold. The king was outraged and ordered the furnace heated seven times hotter than normal. Because of God's infinite protection, Shadrach, Meshach, and Abednego survived unscathed, without a hint of BBQ smell. King Nebuchadnezzar praised God and demanded that no one say anything against their God.

Though I certainly do not desire my girlfriends or husband to reveal my hard-as-Jello abs or my overgrown eyebrows, I value their concern for my character and holding me accountable for my words and actions as a Christian woman. However, whenever I go shopping for a bathing suit, I'll be sure to bring a seven-year-old along and be ready to explain why I have so many craterlike indentions covering my butt and thighs.

The Lord detests lying lips,
    but he delights in people who are trustworthy.

                                    Proverbs 12:22

thou shalt not assume

My husband has a listening disability. If he is watching television or reading a book and I ask him a question or rattle off extremely important information, there is a high probability that my words will fall on deaf ears. Also, he was not born with a gauge inside his body that sends out an alarm and shouts, "Your wife needs help!" if he is caught up in a great magazine article. Even though I may be changing a diaper while our toddler is screaming my name from the backyard and our oldest is in the kitchen trying to make tacos for the family, he hears absolutely nothing.

Men are not mind readers. They need us to ask for their help, and they need to be given specific instructions. Fortunately, no offense is taken when they are confronted with this fact. Men are the first to admit to their lack of the awareness gene.

However, my neighbor wasn't privy to this vital information. She had to leave my son's beach birthday party early, and she left her two children with me. I planned on meeting her at her house by 8:00 p.m. with the rest of the parents. Upon our arrival, she was informed that her son had had a potty accident in the backseat of my car. She rushed into the house and grabbed some clean shorts for her boy and the necessary cleaning supplies for the car. Upon exiting the house, she informed her husband, who was relaxing in his chair with a book, what had happened and returned to the driveway, balancing in her arms the supplies and a wet/dry vacuum.

Her sandy children meandered aimlessly around the yard with the other waiting children while she made Herculean attempts at scouring the soaked seat. She assumed that her husband would realize that things needed to be done — bathing the kids, getting towels and wet clothes put in the laundry room — while she continued her meticulous washing of the backseat. Meanwhile, her husband continued to sit in his comfortable chair and read his novel, while the hum of the vacuum and the chattering of children echoed outside the windows. By 9:00 the cleaning was complete, and everyone had returned home.

I greeted my neighbor the next morning, and she quickly informed me of her disappointment with her husband's lack of help the previous night. After she finished the story, I asked one simple question: "Did you ask him for his help?" She snapped back, "I shouldn't *have* to ask him!" Although this is despairingly true, men need to be asked when there are particular duties that need attention.

No man I know would willingly leap out of his favorite chair, toss his book aside, and rush out to ask, "How can I help you, dear?" Remember, they have a disability, and they need assistance. When asking questions like "Could you please clean out the closets while I am at the six-hour baby shower?" or mentioning the adorable shoes you need to add to your wardrobe, adding a little "sugar" to the request or making the request stark naked is helpful. This is especially true when you're asking questions that have to do with the performance of laborious tasks.

Another friend had decided to run a few errands and leave her husband in charge of their toddling son. When she returned, she noticed that her son was abnormally listless, cranky, and whiney. When she asked if he had fed the boy, her husband replied, "You didn't tell me I needed to feed him."

Hey, he was right.

God is all-powerful and all-knowing. He knows our every move. God knows the number of hairs on our heads. He knows our coming in and our going out, our future and our past. Even God, who is omniscient, desires that our requests be made known to him.

We could go through life avoiding prayer, assuming that since God already knows our needs and knows where and when we need help before we do, prayer is unnecessary. However, to assume this would be absurd. The Bible tells us that God wants us to be specific in our prayers and requests. Although he knows what we're going to ask even before we ask, we need to spend time with God in prayer to seek his wisdom and ask for help.

When we seek God with our requests, I'm confident we'll never find him reclining in a La-Z-Boy, downing Dr. Pepper, and reading a paperback book, completely oblivious to his surroundings. He's perfect!

"Everyone who asks receives; those who seek find; and to those who knock, the door will be opened."

Luke 11:10

the eyes of an invisible dog

No matter how many times I ran through the sprinklers or how many cups of warm lemonade I sold, this particular summer day resonated in my mind as one of the worst days of my childhood. Trying to fry eggs on the sidewalk ended unsatisfactorily, and a play date with Steven D'Braunstein didn't help matters either. His biggest problem was the fact that he was a boy.

We were too hot to ride our bikes and too lazy to climb the avocado trees, and with no central air-conditioning we had the choice of sitting outside in the radiating heat or hiding indoors where box fans blew stale air in circles around our sweaty bodies.

In order to add much-needed excitement to our day I decided that Steven, my brother, and I needed a good laugh. This, I felt, would be a surefire way to break up the monotony that was sucking the very life from us. I pulled out my drawing supplies and began creating a picture. With my wittiest artistic flair, I drew two large circles side by side and placed two smaller circles in the middle of each circle. I carefully colored in the smaller circles, deviously grinned, and held up my masterpiece for the boys to see.

The two of them squirmed and giggled as they began to comprehend what I had created — boobs. I soaked up with delight their laughter and applause, for my plan had worked. However, my joy was short-lived as I heard my mother's footsteps approaching faster than my brain could conjure up a way to purge the pornography.

If I stuffed the paper in my mouth, I wouldn't be able to talk, so I shoved the picture under my behind, hoping for the best outcome. "What are you sitting on?" my mother questioned, while poised in her very best you've-been-up-to-no-good posture. "A picture," I answered. "I didn't want it to blow away so I was acting as a human paperweight." Evidently my explanation didn't ring true, and she asked, "May I see the picture?" As I handed her the drawing, my excuses for the dirty picture kicked into gear. In a very calm, let's-see-if-she-tells-the-truth tone of voice, she asked me to explain what I had drawn.

Like a seasoned professional liar, I told her that the

illustration included two pancakes with a dab of maple syrup in the center. That answer was my first strike. I then explained that the design was of two gigantic eyes from a dog with an invisible body. Strike two. Before any other lame excuse could pour from my mouth, I was marched into the bathroom for the infamous washing of the mouth with a bar of Dial soap as punishment. Suggesting that I clean my hands instead — since they were the culprit, after all — only led to more bubbles on my teeth and taste buds. It was only a suggestion.

Society places lies in two categories — little and white, big and bad. Unfortunately for us, God sees no difference. Whether we are telling the cashier at the department store that we never wore the blouse we are returning for a full refund or explaining to a friend that the reason we cannot attend their baby shower is because our fully functioning child is acutely ill, a lie is a lie. While some people lie to avoid trouble, others lie to impress or to hide the truth from someone or something.

God takes sin seriously — and deceit is an act of sin. When we sin, we hurt God, but when we reach out to Jesus for forgiveness, thankfully he provides it. He does not condemn, pronounce judgment, or seek vengeance; instead, he showers us with sheer, undeserved, unearned, unmerited grace and forgiveness. He loves us through our sin.

Remarkably enough, my savvy drawing skills propelled me into a degree in art from college. Coincidently, in my "life drawing" class I was forced to sketch live naked bodies. For all my efforts in producing lifelike reproductions, I received an A — and no one washed my mouth out with a bar of soap.

Truthful lips endure forever,
but a lying tongue lasts only a moment.

Proverbs 12:19

getting lucky

"You may love the small ones but win the big ones." Fortune cookies have always brought some form of entertainment, and this "fortune" found in a real cookie was no exception. However, instead of being tightly wrapped in the bent shell of a bland-tasting cookie, this "fortune" would have been more apropos if it had been posted in a Vegas casino where the jackpot winner would receive a breast augmentation from a local surgeon.

For a laugh, while in college, I started reading my horoscope. Aside from marking my "love days" in blue pen on the calendar, I didn't take the astrological sign stuff too seriously. However, my friends took astrology way too seriously. Whenever my romantic relationships ended, they attributed the breakup to the fact that our birth signs were incompatible. However, throwing caution to the wind and risking that we would soon be sucked into a vortex of cosmic chaos involving human-headed horses and naked men with water jugs, I married a man whose birth sign is the same as mine.

A well-documented fact is that celebrities and athletes are known for having superstitious habits. Cameron Diaz wears a necklace given to her by a friend, which is supposed to ward off the effects of aging. Plastic surgeons would be out of business if antiaging was conveniently packaged in the wearing of a gold necklace. However, the supernatural is manifested only if the necklace doesn't give you a rash or turn your neck green.

Major League baseball player Darin Erstad wears around his neck a leather pouch filled with a combination of minerals that are supposed to ward off injuries and slumps. If his parents had known that magic was housed in a bag of dust, they could have saved thousands of dollars on batting lessons and personal trainers.

These minerals and mind games are no more effective than wishing someone good luck. Before friends or family members begin a new journey, start a new job, or drive to the hospital to have a baby, people often wish them "good luck." However, no form of good wishing, wearing the same shirt as long as your team is winning, knocking on wood, or delving into the world of horoscopes, tarot cards, or palm readers can change the world in which we live.

Even some men whose stories are told in the Bible thought that a medium could give them creditable guidance. King Saul, although strictly forbidden by God, went to a medium in the hope that she would speak encouraging words about the army coming against him. Saul was terrified because God had taken his Spirit from him due to his continued disobedience. Even so, he sought God's guidance, but God was silent. He attempted to hear from God through prophets, but they were mute. He asked God to appear to him in a dream, but God remained invisible. Saul couldn't even text God because God would delete the message.

That is when Saul, alone, terrified, and desperate, ran into the tent of Madame Doomsayer, grabbed the crystal ball, and hoped for the best. However, she brought him no comfort because all she did was repeat God's message that he was no longer with Saul and that the kingdom would be yanked from his hands and given to David.

With God as the center of our lives, we know that he is sovereign over all things, is in control of all things, and allows all things. God's children do not need charms, fortune tellers, or tarot cards. Because of the redemptive work of Jesus Christ, we have the omnipotent, omniscient, all-wise God as our Father who loves us beyond our capacity to understand and with whom we have a personal relationship. He even brings together people with the same astrological birth sign because he has the uncanny ability to halt the beginnings of all life-sucking vortexes.

> *We know that in all things God works for the good of those who love him, who have been called according to his purpose.*
>
> *Romans 8:28*

frog hunt

Frustration ran high as the afternoon came. Our children melted into the couch. They were officially comatose. Determined to get them out of the house, I shut off the television, clapped my hands twice, and barked out orders in hopes of summoning them to an alert state. "Get your flip-flops on. We're going on a frog hunt."

Knowing that if I used words like *hike* and *nature*, a growl might ensue, I chose alluring words like *flip-flops* and *frogs* to spark their curiosity.

After gathering my troops along with a couple of neighbor kids and my niece, we piled into the car and headed up the hill to find a creek and capture frogs. Questions flew as we turned and twisted through the small hill that sits directly north of our house. I kept the information brief and minimal because I had no idea where we were going and what we would find once we got there. Besides, not knowing was an integral part of the adventure.

I had gotten information about the location of the creek from my girlfriend, who lives near the canyon. After her clear directions, I pictured a short, meandering dirt trail leading to a moss-lined creek that babbled and bobbed along, buzzing with nature and bustling with critters needing their happy habitat interrupted by seven zealous children.

Keep that thought.

"Where's the creek?" was the common question to which I didn't have the answer. I had taken a class in college called "Understanding the Environment (I needed the units), and so I recalled what little information I surprisingly still had stored in my head and concluded that the dark-green vegetation a few yards off the trail was a sign of a water source. But the barbwire fence and overgrown brush surrounding the water source indicated that entering the creek world required leather gloves, a machete, and steel-toe boots. Flip-flops, shorts, and toddlers were utterly insufficient.

The animated frog–catching photo in my mind burst. "Let's check out what's just around this bend," I shouted as my mother stopped a bike rider with questions about the location and distance of the so-called creek. Hopeful answers kept us moving in anticipation of the frogs and wildlife. "Maybe it's just around *this* bend," I hollered to the troops more than once.

By that time the afternoon sun had blazed through our skin and the dust had coated our bare feet. If not for the determination and energy of the little ones, I would have turned back and driven to the nearest ice cream store, bellied up to the counter, ordered our treats, and called it an afternoon.

Each bend led to another stretch of path, and by now we were twenty minutes into our "adventure." While vacillating between turning back and moving forward, I heard the neighbor boy shout, "Here it is!" Ah, music to my ears. We all screamed and ran so we could begin our follies in the water. To our dismay, the creek did not babble, and the creatures evidently had all run for cover at the first shriek of human voices.

In our dusty flip-flops, we crouched on our haunches and hushed our voices, hoping to witness some sort of movement. Upon closer investigation, there on the elongated blades of grass we noticed tiny frogs. While cupping our hands around their bodies, we slid them off one by one and plopped them into a jar filled with a touch of pond water and stuffed with grass. By golly, we were catching frogs!

In between frog catching we looked for tadpoles, we found raccoon tracks, one of the children peed in the bushes, someone got a thorn in his toe, another slipped in the slime, and another lost his "flip" in the sticky, unrelenting goop that lined the edge of the water. Eventually our adventure came to an end. After we caught and released eight slimy frogs, we made our way back to the car. Since I was as unprepared as a mother giving birth thirty days early, the nine of us wet our dusty throats by sharing sips from one small bottle of water. We then stopped at the convenience store for a well-deserved round of Slurpees.

God gives all of us roads to travel. We make the choice whether to take the road he designed for us or to tread the path we chose on our own. Sometimes his road seems hard and hilly. There are bends that lead to more curves and hills. At times we want to pull out a machete and chop down the dense brush in the hope of creating a shortcut.

Persisting down God's path leads to bends in the road that make us stronger and hills that build our commitment and create tenacity. God never promised that his road would be easy, but he did promise a path that would lead us to eternal life with him in heaven.

I know that God holds our hands through this entire journey we call life, even if the path is dusty and covered in frog slime — but for that we have showers and baths.

> *"This is what the Lord says —*
> *your Redeemer, the Holy One of Israel:*
> *I am the Lord your God,*
> *who teaches you what is best for you,*
> *who directs you in the way you should go."*
>
> *Isaiah 48:17*

shower with a friend

The pungent smell of shaving cream permeates the shower walls as my two-year-old heaps the foamy goop into his tiny palms and "paints" the glass doors of the shower. I never shower alone if my youngest child is awake. If he is not enjoying the warm mistiness with me, he is pushing his pants down on the other side of the sliding glass door while screaming, "Me! Me! I get in!" If I ignore him, he will reach into the drawer by the sink and find my hairbrush with the wooden handle to bang on the glass door.

This makes a fabulous sound in a wet environment with lots of tile and no sound absorption.

The reverberation makes my teeth feel like they are

popping out of my gums. After he gains entrance into the shower, the challenge comes when my legs need shaving. I have to hurl my leg over his head and balance my toes on the wall while clumps of shaving cream drop on his wet head. Inevitably, a glob slips to his face and I have to quickly give him a good rinse. They don't make tear-free shaving cream. I can't imagine why. Perhaps if enough people start shaving their eyebrows, the need will become more apparent.

Moms never seem to be able to do anything alone. We could be on our way to a needlepoint convention, and someone would beg to tag along. Even going to the bathroom elicits an entourage of visitors asking insignificant questions they think need immediate answers or juice cups calling for quick refills. There is good news to all of this, thankfully — if you're an optimistic sort, that is. Scientists say the happiest people spend the least amount of time alone. Does that mean I should be sad and glum while my kids are napping? Do these scientists have toddlers?

Many things make me happy, and finding time to be alone is one of them. There are, without a doubt, times when I'm alone too much and miss the flurry of family, but the importance of getting time alone is essential.

In the moments when I allow my brain to shut off, God is able to speak and I'm able to listen. Giving him the opportunity to meet me in a quiet place, free from household disturbances, is rejuvenating and affords me the best opportunity to meet with him in prayer.

In my prayer time, I begin with thanksgiving, for it is through this process I am reminded of all my blessings. Next I confess my character flaws and let him know how desperately I need his help. Then I inform him of my needs and let him know that I truly want his will in all things — and then I express trust in his perfect timing. God is omniscient. He knows our every need, and yet he still desires that we ask. I end with a praise song, one that is usually stuck in my head from hearing it on the radio, or I fumble through the words of a song I thought I knew but have to fill in the blanks as I go.

Spending time with God in prayer is like making a deposit into our spiritual lives. Thankfully, the return is tenfold. We are able to withdraw blessings, peace, hope, and a significant relationship with our loving Father in heaven. As far as the showering goes, I've learned to avoid having to share the showerhead with others by locking the doors. I know — I'm a tad slow.

Very early in the morning, while it was still dark, Jesus got up, left the house and went off to a solitary place, where he prayed.

Mark 1:35

driving charlie

Charlie stood at the edge of the entrance to the housing complex and the busy road. I had to make a wide left turn to avoid hitting him. Decked out in orange Crocs and gray socks and holding a yellow briefcase, he hobbled toward my car as if to stop me from arriving at my destination. The cane he used was aluminum, and his dark hair was side-swiped with gray. I assumed he needed directions, and while my youngest boy, entranced by a handheld video game, ignored the situation, I stopped.

I pushed the button, which allowed the car window to go down so I could give the necessary directions. Giving directions is my specialty. To my surprise, he didn't need directions. "Could you give me a lift to the bus stop?" he asked while approaching my window. Before I could conjure up a proper excuse for why I couldn't allow a strange man into my car, the word "Sure" spilled from my mouth. "Great!" he replied. I touched my lips wondering, *Did I just agree to take a perfect stranger to the bus stop?*

As he hobbled painfully toward my car, my mind immediately went into "stranger danger" mode, and my first thought was, I could take him down if I had to. I was twice his size and without physical limitations. Secondly, I began rummaging through an inventory of items lying in and around the seats of my car, deciding which ones could be used for defense in an extreme case. On a certain level, I knew we were in no immediate danger; nonetheless, I had to be prepared.

I had a cap gun, a battery charger for my mobile phone, a bungee cord, and a bottle of water. At the very least, my four-year-old could hold the gun to the stranger's head while I wrapped the bungee cord around his neck, keeping it snug to the headrest. I reasoned that the battery charger could impale his hands while I poured the bottled water on his head. My fear quickly turned to empathy as Charlie struggled his way into the seat next to me because he was unable to bend his legs. Any fear I had of my stranger quickly vanished.

He began by introducing himself and explaining how he ended up depending on the mercy of other people. His wife, who normally took him to work, had exited the house quickly because she was running late. He assured her that his battery-powered chair would take him to the bus stop so that he could get to the nearby junior college where he was teaching a political science course. When he hopped aboard his chair, much to his chagrin he discovered that the battery was dead. He would have to rely on the goodness of man to escort him to the bus stop.

By the end of his story, I had decided to drive past the bus stop and go directly to the college. He was obviously grateful. This was my opportunity to help a man desperate to get to work on time.

As we drove the six miles to the college, I learned that Charlie was a native of India. He had been diagnosed with juvenile arthritis at age fourteen, and an Indian surgeon had prescribed bed rest for one year — an ill-advised solution as it turned out, for during that year his bones stiffened, resulting in his present condition.

I sprinkled our conversation with words about Jesus whenever I could. He didn't engage me in conversations about Jesus as I had hoped he would, and he was quick to find fault in "a God who would allow so much suffering." I did my best to offer a reason, but his denial was profound. He actually thought that given the chance, he could do better than God. I bid him a great day with God's blessing as we shook hands.

God prompts us to do certain things often at inconvenient times. He tugs at our subconscious with a persistent demand we can either choose to obey or to ignore. I have experienced my share of ignoring God's tugs, and the guilt feels uncomfortable. At that moment I wasn't about to allow my selfish needs to interfere with a tug from God. The repercussions would surely manifest themselves, so I chose to be obedient.

Although I may never know what effect my obedience had on Charlie, I do know I experienced great joy. Chances are I am going to miss God's tug again at some point, but hopefully I'll be obedient more often than not. I also hope the Lord knows that I don't share my ice cream.

"Truly I tell you, whatever you did for one of the least of these brothers and sisters of mine, you did for me."

Matthew 25:40

circus acts

At some point in our lives, we have looked at our reflections in the mirror and found something worthy of a complaint. My mirror image shows ugly blotches, blemishes, and brown spots, leaving me wishing they would find themselves another home.

However, I do take full responsibility. Lathering on the baby oil and sitting on top of foil in the sun for six hours has consequences. Sunscreen was a four-letter word during my teen years, and if a dermatologist had looked close enough, they would have seen the reflection of a sunlamp and tanning bed bulb. Motherhood has also left some unflattering results — squiggly wormlike marks on my hips, unwelcome shrinkage in the bra area, and dimples in places where dimples aren't cute.

Finding fault in my physical appearance was an everyday occurrence until I was channel-hopping one evening and came across a medical show featuring two sisters who could have been a must-see at an old-fashioned circus sideshow where the freakish and unfit were on display. Conjoined in the womb, these modern-day Siamese twins were attached at the topside of their heads. One of the girls had to carry her shorter sister on a metal tray with wheels. Although not hideous by any means, I suppose that throughout their forty years on the earth, they have endured countless stares, gasps, and the prick of fingers pointing in their direction.

The gentleman interviewing the sisters asked questions, and they quietly responded. As the interview drew to a close, he finally asked the question that had plagued me during the entire program. "If you knew that you could be separated, would you make the choice to do so?"

To my amazement, they simultaneously responded with a resounding no. They explained that their lives are full and that there are so many things they can do in spite of their limitations. They have a loving family and have shared many memorable experiences together. The sisters ended their interview with this humble statement: "This is how God created us, and we would never want to change something that God made."

My heart sank with disappointment and shame as I pondered my mental list of complaints. The list was long. Through the story of these sisters' lives, I realized that

God made me exactly the way he intended — including blotches, blemishes, and brown spots.

God's desire is that we focus on pleasing and loving him. This allows us to love others as he intended us to love them and to love ourselves in spite of our defects. Through giving love to others and receiving love from God, we can travel a scenic road that features God as our guide. How great is that?

> *I praise you because I am fearfully and wonderfully made;*
> *your works are wonderful,*
> *I know that full well.*
>
> Psalm 139:14

mistaken identity

I invited a Doberman pinscher into the backseat of my car only after recognizing that she was my girlfriend's dog and was three blocks from her home. Without a thought I pulled over, rolled down my window, and shouted, "Heidi, get in the car!" She glanced in my direction and ignored my command and continued sniffing the essence emitting from a nearby bush. Frustrated, I got out of the car, stomping my feet as I drew closer to the unleashed dog.

If I could get her into the car, I could drive her home. I wasn't about to park the car and hoof my way to her house, hoping she would follow, because any amount of running or sweating would mean that the hairspray locking each strand of hair perfectly into place would break loose. That road I would *not* travel.

I got close enough, grabbed her collar, and dragged the unyielding canine off the sidewalk. Even though Dobermans make fantastic watchdogs and often show aggression, I had no fear. Heidi was a gentle, loving dog. We had a relationship.

I motioned her to the open door, expressing reprimand with each tug. She leaped into the backseat as I quickly shut the door, checking my hair for correct stiffness and my brow for moisture. Although I knew my girlfriend wasn't home, I planned to open the side gate and return Heidi to the backyard, where she belonged.

When I opened the back door of my car, Heidi jumped out and walked toward the yard. At the next moment, while inhaling a scent from the base of a tree, she did something very strange. She ambled closer to the trunk of the tree, lifted her leg, and exposed plumbing that belonged distinctly to the male variety of Doberman. I had the wrong dog. The real Heidi barked upon our arrival, and I ran back to my car, fearing that my mistaken identity would result in teeth marks in bare places.

People often make mistakes. I wish I was mistaken for Jennifer Aniston. People would run up to me at the grocery store and beg for an autograph — and then I'd have to show them my Costco card to prove my true identity. "Oh!" they would say. "You could be her twin."

"I know," I would reply. "People tell me that all the time."

In actuality, people tell me I could be Alan Ruck's sister.

spilt milk

He was the best friend of Ferris Bueller in *Ferris Bueller's Day Off*. I don't find this to be much of a compliment.

Unfortunately, people harbor some misconceptions about me. They mistake me for another one of those "born agains" who points her judgmental finger and reports all of their wrongdoings to Jesus, Mary, Joseph, and anyone else who is willing to listen. They mistake me for someone who is vain because I enjoy getting my hair highlighted and having a pedicure every other month. They mistake me for someone who has life wired when in reality I wish I could have my appendix start to burst, which would cause me to be hospitalized for days — just so I could get a break from motherhood. They mistake me for someone who has a problem with self-control when they see me escorting my child out of the toy store by forcefully grabbing his arm. They fail to see the previous few seconds when he scratched his brother's face, which drew blood, and the child who shrieked seven times, "Buy me a toy!"

I, too, am guilty of misjudgments and misunderstandings. I keep reminding myself that in light of my misgivings, I have neither space nor authority to judge others. Only God in heaven has the nameplate inscribed with "Judge over All" — and, thankfully, he likes my highlights.

"Do not judge, or you too will be judged. For in the same way you judge others, you will be judged, and with the measure you use, it will be measured to you."

Matthew 7:1 – 2

you're hired!

My husband stood outside, waiting anxiously as I slowly pulled the car into the driveway. While holding the baby, he strolled toward the car, grinning. With tears in my eyes, I rolled down the window, turned my head toward him, and said, "I got the job." He smiled, and I cried. These were not tears of joy. Normally the phrase "You're hired!" brings happiness; however, after having been a stay-at-home mom, these words brought sadness.

My husband and I had decided it was imperative that I return to teaching in order to help make ends meet financially. I called the one connection I had at the school district, all the while asking God to help me through this frightening step. After my first interview, I was told I was hired. All of my personal requests, which included insurance benefits and the time to finish up another part-time job, were willingly met. There was no doubt I wasn't the one in control. I drove home that afternoon, feeling sad for my family and all that was going to transpire within the next week. The one bright spot was that after years of jeans, a T-shirt, and flip-flops, I still knew how to throw together a suitable outfit for an interview and drape on a dashing demeanor.

In order for me to work, some problems needed solving. First, my oldest was in school full-time and my going back to work meant finding day care for my nine-month-old and switching my five-year-old to full day preschool and figuring out what to do with him on the two days he didn't have class. I also knew that getting up at 5:30 in the morning and taking over for a teacher in the middle of the year were going to be challenges.

Every inch of me resented having to step into a classroom again. I wanted to do the right thing, but I was having a difficult time extinguishing my bitterness. The light at the end of the tunnel was the fact that school ended in the middle of June, and we were approaching mid-February. *Only four months*, I kept telling myself, *and then I'll be home for the summer.* Faithfully I kept giving my stress to God and asking him to help me through all the changes taking place in our family. In a short time, every detail was worked out completely. My mother-in-law offered to watch the baby, and my girlfriend volunteered to help out with my older son.

A web of excitement began to weave within me, along with a feeling of gratification that I was able to help my husband in providing for our family. While continuing to work even harder at getting his business off the ground, he had to do some of the "mommy" stuff in the morning and step into the carpool role. I knew that my going back to work full-time was far from his first choice, and because I knew that, it made the change easier.

The students were receptive and the staff was remarkable. Within the first two weeks, a small note written by second grade hands was slipped onto my desk. It read, "There once was a little girl. Her teacher's name was Mrs. Vujnov. Her teacher was very nice to her. She wishes that her teacher was her mom. By Morgan."

Although my family needed to make adjustments, I was exactly where I needed to be — even if I did cry the whole way there.

"For I know the plans I have for you," declares the LORD, "plans to prosper you and not to harm you, plans to give you hope and a future."

Jeremiah 29:11

meanest mom in the world

I find no offense in the title "Meanest Mom in the World,"
since the name was self-selected. Conveniently, though,
I am married to the meanest dad in the world. Since our
children do not understand why they are forbidden to do
anything, with anyone, at anytime, but must first acquire
permission, our titles fit perfectly.

When I disagree with one of their requests, my response is, "I know — I am the meanest mom in the world."
Rolling eyes and skeptical head shaking are the typical
reaction. If our children were able to make all their own
decisions, the outcome would result in broken bones,

sleepless nights, and our mandatory enrollment in a five-month parenting class.

Instead of participation in safe activities like poking a bug's backside or throwing handfuls of dirt at the dog, our youngest prefers climbing the playset ladder to dizzying heights. He proceeds to point out crows and sparrows chirping and cawing atop his castle while balancing on one foot and leaning over the railing. A quick motherly whisk off the playset gives way to wailing. Restrictions of that caliber render my title appropriate.

Another child loves to saunter into the house, ready to strike up a game of baseball with any breathing creature. Complete with cleats, aluminum bat, hard ball, and batting helmet, he acts as if our entryway is brick dust, and the pitcher's mound sits somewhere behind the loveseat. When I drag the items back to the garage, I instantly become the meanest mom in the world. After all, only nice mommies allow their sons to engage in a "swing and a miss" in the middle of the living room.

Our oldest boy asks if he can have a five-friend sleepover, complete with ice cream floats and family-size bags of chips, on a school night. After his request is rejected, his breathy noises, furrowed brow, and pout makes any mom second-guess her decision. Standing my ground, I come back with, "It sure is hard when your mother is the meanest in the world."

Our daughter constantly asks if she can wear flip-flops and sweatpants to church. Saying no gets the head drop and boneless arms. When I serve the offer to trade me for a kinder, sweeter mother, she never takes the bait. Instead, her monotone voice replies, "Not funny, Mom."

Our children do not always enjoy being disciplined or told they cannot do something that they find appropriate. However, I do know they respect our decisions as parents — or at least they will when they have children of their own. Structure, curfews, and restrictions seem like four-letter words for most children, but studies show that children desire sameness and continuity, guidelines and limits. When left to their own wills and desires, kids will inevitably fall into trouble. Setting borders and disciplining children are the very best things we can do for them. Moans, groans, and flops cannot sway our decisions. Our goal is to be the best parents, not the best friends.

When God says no to our requests, we often react with our own outpouring of pouts, whines, and wails. God has a bird's-eye view of the big picture, and his job is to protect us, just as ours is to protect our children. Hebrews 12:11 reads, "No discipline seems pleasant at the time, but painful. Later on, however, it produces a harvest of righteousness and peace for those who have been trained by it." We must trust in God's decisions for our lives. Only he knows the end from the beginning.

Having friends sleep over and stay up late chomping on chips until 2:00 a.m. and slurping on ice cream floats is my idea of a great time — just not on a school night. After all, I am the meanest mom in the world.

Discipline your children, and they will give you peace;
they will bring you the delights you desire.

Proverbs 29:17

warning signs

Warning signs are everywhere. They deliver such messages as "Do Not Enter," "Yield to Oncoming Traffic," "One Way," and "Hitchhikers May Be Escaping Inmates."

Yes, really.

The most overdone warning occurs when red lights flash, bells sound, and a wooden arm falls across the street, blocking any interaction between your car and the speeding train. But still some fail to heed the obvious warnings.

Every Monday during the school year, my daughter coaxes her grandma into an after-school date for homework help and "quiet time" free from any and all younger brothers. Before dropping her off, we drive to a local restaurant to purchase a Philly cheesesteak sandwich so that my mom doesn't have to create a meal.

Just like every other Monday, I parked near the front entrance and exited the car to place the order while my daughter stayed in the car. As the door closed, the radio blared, and all communication from the world outside the four metal doors was quickly eliminated.

As I was in the process of paying for the sandwich, my daughter appeared suddenly at my side. Wondering what warranted such a sudden appearance, I asked, "Do you need something?" She just stared and didn't answer. Teenagers are a mysterious earth form.

Since she didn't answer, I stood there, wondering what was different about this day as opposed to every other Monday when she would stay in the car and anticipate the arrival of her warm sandwich. "Did something scare you?" I queried, attempting to discern why she was standing so close to me. Blank stare. "Did someone come to the car window?" Same blank stare. "Did you miss me?" I ventured. This time the blank stare changed to a look that said, "As if!" At least this time there was a glimmer of a reaction.

Abandoning the task of ever finding out why she got out of the car, I turned my question to the practical realm and asked, "Where are my keys?" My daughter's eyes enlarged, her hand went to her mouth, and she raced out the door as a feeling of dread surfaced in my gut. I peered out from the window, gazing at my daughter frantically dashing around to all the car doors and trying each one of them but getting the same results. They were all locked.

She returned to the restaurant, showing the signs of a contrite heart — alright, maybe not contrite, but there was a smattering of remorse in her expression. "Didn't you hear that the radio was on or that there was a distinct ding, ding, ding, ding, dinging when you opened the door?" I questioned with some signs of frustration. "No!" was my daughter's one-word response. Of course she didn't. While she enjoyed the first half of her sandwich, I phoned my mother to ask for a ride home.

At times, God asks us the same question when we get into trouble. "Didn't you hear the ding, ding, ding found in my Word that would have prevented you from rebelling against my will?" I'm sure we would have answered yes, but just like my daughter, we chose to ignore the warning.

Look at David, who knew only too well God's admonishment against adultery. Yet when his eyes gazed on the beautiful Bathsheba, he didn't pay attention to the ding, ding, dinging. What about Judas, the betrayer of Jesus. Jesus, during the Last Supper, said that one of the twelve would betray him. That ding, ding, dinging was so loud that the warning should have been impossible to ignore, but ignore the warning is just what Judas did — and that act of disobedience cost him his life.

Just like David, Judas, my daughter, and most of us,

we don't want to suffer the consequences when we ignore God's warning signals. However, God allows us to suffer the consequences so that our ears will be more carefully tuned to his ding, ding, dingings in the future.

The following week I was again coaxed into a dinner-out purchase, and again my daughter chose to wait in the car. When she appeared suddenly, just as I was about to pay the bill, I asked with trepidation, "Where are my keys?" With a gleeful smile, she dangled them in front of my face and replied, "Right here!" This time she didn't miss the ding, ding, ding.

The precepts of the Lord are right,
   giving joy to the heart.
The commands of the LORD are radiant,
   giving light to the eyes. . . .
By them your servant is warned;
   in keeping them there is great reward.

                              Psalm 19:8, 11

behaving badly

There is a small window of time when our family can enjoy a dinner replete with friendly servers and menus we can hold in our hands. When that window closes, some of us transform into creatures with growling stomachs as alien beings slither around our bellies and brain. Some become unfocused and whiney. I may be one of those people.

One evening my husband and I were driving to a nearby restaurant with our four children safely seat belted in the backseat. On this particular occasion, I drew the short straw and was driving. Timewise we were doing fine — until we became stuck at a left-turn signal that seemed to be taking an unusually long time to turn green. I sensed that our "window" was getting dangerously close to shutting when two of the four children stated that they were hungry.

As we sat at the signal, I noticed the opposite signal turning yellow, which could only result in our light soon turning green. With my foot in position to accelerate through the turn, I detected a band of boisterous junior highers walking through the crosswalk with absolutely no regard to the fact that their light had turned red and our left-turn arrow had turned green.

I immediately took offense at the attitude of teens as I envisioned the hideous beings budding inside the confines of our car if we missed our opportunity to turn left into the restaurant parking lot and had to undergo another round of turn signals and idling cars.

A courteous driver would have acknowledged the giggling girls, rolled her eyes, ignored the glaring green arrow, and allowed the teens to saunter through the red light, laughing and carrying on. However, I was in no mood to be courteous. I honked the horn seconds before they passed in front of our car, and then I accelerated through the green arrow, interrupting their leisurely stroll with my car. As they shrieked, stopping dead in their tracks in the middle of the crosswalk, I broke out into a sweat and sunk down into my seat, and I quickly settled into a parking spot, miserable and embarrassed, for I realized that my children had been watching my every move.

Unfortunately, I set three examples that night: true

dislike for junior high girls who had no consideration for pedestrian laws; lack of self-control; and gross impatience with safety as an issue. It doesn't get much worse than that! Immediately I felt awful and explained to my kids that what I did had been very wrong.

Parents lead by example, no matter how many times we wish the adage "Do as I say and not as I do" could actually stick. Jesus knew he had to lead his people by example. Although Jesus was without sin, he was constantly judged by how he reacted to situations he encountered while he lived on earth. His actions would be scrutinized, his love would be modeled, his sacrifices taken into account, his pleasure measured, his perseverance praised, his strength revered, his struggles shared, his mercy gauged — and we, his children, would be expected to follow his example.

Our children follow by example, which is a scary thought. Our outbursts, sarcasm, mishaps, misjudgments, and falters are constantly being scrutinized, as well as our joys, humility, friendships, and attitude. We lead by example as our children follow. Thankfully, we have God's Word as a guide, with step-by-step instructions. If only there were more pictures. I need the visual.

In everything set them an example by doing what is good. In your teaching show integrity, seriousness and soundness of speech that cannot be condemned.

Titus 2:7–8

frying eggs

Getting an F for the day in PE wasn't something I had planned on. In actuality, I didn't mind dressing out and getting physical. I'm weird that way. That is not why I failed.

Our PE uniforms were ordered straight from "Reform School Uniforms Plus," circa 1955. The top half was a T-shirt — with gold and white stripes and a sexy stretch-polyester collar. The bottom half was fashioned into gold poly-blend shorts. The two halves were joined by a sweet ring of elastic, making the entire outfit one piece, gathered snugly around the waist.

One cool morning, we all stood on a grassy knoll outside the locker room dressed in our fashionable PE uniforms and waiting for instructions. No one would ever inform the teacher that the weather was uncomfortably cold because inevitably she would make us run a lap to warm up. Our wait grew dull, so I yelled loud enough for everyone to hear, "Guess what I am?" as I plopped on my backside in the grass and began to flinch. The flinching turned to twitching and the twitching to convulsing. Then, I flipped over and landed on my front side. I convulsed for a few more seconds and then stopped and leaped to my feet, stating, "So what am I?" My riddle-challenged friends had no idea, so I answered, "A fried egg!" Most of them laughed and requested an encore. As I was finishing up the encore flip, our PE teacher appeared. I willingly jumped up to begin our lesson as she pointed at me and said, "That's an F for the day."

Before I could fully comprehend what had just happened, we were rushed off into teams for basketball. I couldn't understand what I had done to deserve failure before class officially began, so I walked with her at the end of PE class and asked for a deeper explanation. Her information was shocking. She noted that as she was leaving the locker room she had witnessed my twitching and convulsing on the grass. Her assumption was that I was imitating an epileptic having a seizure — an inexcusable act. My jaw dropped as I composed my explanation. She listened and smiled when I told her that I was imitating an egg frying in a pan. However, the F remained. Perception and reality had a tumultuous tangle.

In the book of Genesis, Joseph experienced the consequences of a misconception — although his incident never involved eggs. Even though a slave, Joseph was entrusted with everything Potiphar owned. Since Joseph was the biblical equivalent of Brad Pitt, Potiphar's wife taunted him daily with sexual advances. He kept refusing, so one day she surprised him in an abandoned room, grabbed him by his cloak, and attempted to seduce him. In his haste to get away, Joseph left behind his cloak as he ran out the door.

Potiphar's wife told everyone, including her husband, that Joseph had left his cloak in her room because he was seducing her and she was screaming and fighting off his advances — and so he forgot his robe as he made a quick exit. Potiphar fumed and wouldn't listen to Joseph's explanation. Once again a dichotomy between perception and reality existed; however, whereas I was given an F for my fried-egg interpretation, Joseph was thrown into prison.

God knew my intentions, just as he knew Joseph's. Because of Joseph's obedience to God's laws, he was later placed in command of Pharaoh's palace, was given Pharaoh's signet ring, and was dressed in robes of fine linen and draped with gold chains. As for me, after diligently dressing out each day for PE and avoiding all stand-up comedy during periods of waiting for our teacher to arrive, my final grade was an A minus.

spilt milk

"I the LORD search the heart
*   and examine the mind,*
to reward everyone according to their conduct,
*   according to what their deeds deserve."*

Jeremiah 17:10

pity? party of two

My girlfriend and I decided to have a pity party one afternoon. Instead of drowning ourselves in cigarettes and cocktails, we gorged on diet soda and Nacho Cheese Doritos. She started the party by revealing the frustration she feels as she cares for her eighty-two-year-old, non-English speaking, live-in father-in-law. That morning, she discovered his two-day-old urine-saturated pants in the bottom of his hamper. Last week, he fell into their Jacuzzi — and my friend, who was fully clothed, had to play lifeguard.

Also, when she volunteers to be a field trip chaperone for one of her four children, she has to either call a sitter or take her father-in-law along. He rides shotgun. He is included in every family vacation, dinner out, shopping experience, and church service. He doesn't eat unless someone prepares his meals, and then he needs encouragement to sit down and eat.

And that wasn't the half of it.

After listening to her, I felt as though the complaints I had brought to our party belonged somewhere behind the sofa. However, to stay in the game, I took a deep breath and spewed some garden-variety gripes.

My groans grew from the fact that my only girl wants to wear only boy clothes, and that my youngest threw my favorite watch into the public restroom toilet and laughed as I stuck my arm into the water to retrieve it. Feeling like I needed to score some more points, I recalled how I had to chauffer my mother to appliance and furniture stores, midafternoon, in August, with a two-year-old and three-month-old in tow.

My additions to the pity party were child's play.

After venting our complaints, we discussed the things people do that are particularly bothersome. Included in our verbal list were people who clip their fingernails during church and the times we have to stand at the end of a five-person bathroom line with our four-year-old holding her crotch — while no one offers to let you go to the front of the line. In addition, neither of us can understand how a three-inch-long hair can suddenly burst out on your chin overnight.

The confetti was thrown, and our party ended. As I reflected on our complaints, I was reluctant to realize that, try as I might to appreciate all the ways I've been blessed, I catch myself sitting down to a round of the "Why me?" game more often than I should.

Feeling sorry for myself momentarily can be cleansing, and God recognizes the legitimacy of my feelings. In the garden of Gethsemane on the night before Jesus was crucified, he had every right to feel sorry for himself. While in the throes of his excruciating misery, he called out to God, "My Father, if it is possible, may this cup be taken from me." I can just imagine a pause, a sigh, and then a heartfelt surrender as he continued, "Yet not as I will, but as you will" (Matthew 26:39). Nothing we experience can be compared to what Jesus experienced, but because he walked on earth as a human being, he understands.

Invite God to your next pity party, but don't expect it to last very long. I've been told that he always brings a bowl of blessings. Party over!

May our Lord Jesus Christ himself and God our Father, who loved us and by his grace gave us eternal encouragement and good hope, encourage your hearts and strengthen you in every good deed and word.

2 Thessalonians 2:16 – 17

high-speed chase

When I wasn't riding my moped or my brother's single-cylinder, five-speed Yamaha street motorcycle to work, I drove my mother's metallic-brown, fastback Ford Mustang with bucket seats and a sweet stereo system. This car was fast and smooth. Needless to say, I was the envy of every boy in my neighborhood.

I mostly worked nights, since going to school got in the way of any type of day job. This worked out perfectly, since the roller rink where I was employed didn't open until 3:00 p.m. on weekdays. After closing out the snack bar one night and saying good night to the last customer to leave, I strapped on my skates and challenged two male floor guards to a five-lap race around the rink. The manager turned the music up loud as we bolted from the starting line, and by lap four I was well ahead of the men, and I beat them to the finish line.

After congratulatory high fives, the two floor guards challenged me to a rematch the following day. Wet with sweat, and feeling overconfident, I gladly agreed. I then gathered my keys and a cold drink and headed for home in my mother's car, feeling fairly satisfied with myself.

After exiting the parking lot and turning left toward my home, a barren street with few signals sprawled out before me. The first signal brought a red light. Sensing that the person in the car next to mine was staring at me, I turned my head to look. There in the driver's seat sat one of the guys I had just thumped in the roller-skating race. He signaled for me to roll down my window, and he challenged me to a race — this time with cars. I laughed, staring at his Volkswagen Bug, topless and in need of new tires, and revved the engine of the Mustang to indicate "Race on!" When the red signal turned bright green, we floored the accelerators of our cars and sped down the road.

Within seconds, I was ahead in the competition. However, my elation was quickly deflated as red flashing lights appeared in my rearview mirror. My first thought was to ditch the black-and-white car that was fast approaching my rear bumper. If I could make a quick getaway, I would (1) avoid a speeding ticket and reckless driving violation and (2) avoid having to tell my mother I was using her car for racing purposes. Still thinking I was ahead of the officer and well on my way to avoiding a ticket, I turned quickly into the quiet neighborhood where a friend of mine lived. She was always up late at night watching recordings of afternoon soaps on the TV in her living room. Surely the officer would never follow me there.

The tires screeched with every turn, and finally my friend's house came into view. I raced up the driveway, slammed on the brakes, killed the engine, leaped from the driver's seat, and ran to the front door. Just as I was about to dash through the doorway, the black-and-white car appeared curbside. My shoulders dropped as I turned to see the officer approaching.

The officer was calm. He acted as though he had been dealing with speeding teens all night. He asked me about the events, and I simply told the truth — that I was racing my friend and got scared when I saw the police car. He smiled and sent me on my way, asking me to promise to (1) never race again and (2) never try to outrun a cop. With no prodding, I gratefully agreed.

I deserved a ticket. I deserved a tongue-lashing. I deserved a reprimand. I deserved consequences, but instead I received mercy.

God is the ultimate mercy granter. I am a sinner who constantly makes mistakes; I am a repeat offender who deserves to suffer the consequences. I fail God numerous times, wreaking havoc on my life as well as on the lives of others. I violate. I discriminate. I isolate myself from God. I ignore God's calling and seek my own way of doing things. I deserve punishment, but God gives me mercy. How great is our God!

I can honestly say that, to this day, I've never raced any-one in my car or tried to ditch a cop. I kept my promise, but I can still gain a fair amount of speed on my roller skates. Want to race?

Those who conceal their sins do not prosper,
but those who confess and renounce them find mercy.

Proverbs 28:13

mr. and mrs. bird

The bird in the tree outside my front door must be married. It would be hard for her to be shacking up with some guy bird, since there is only room in the nest for her feathered rump and the four eggs she sits on daily. Also, she obviously has no degree in architectural design, given the fact that the nest appears to be flimsy and shallow.

Each morning, she flits around with another bird, which is hopefully the father of her chicks — although she doesn't wear a ring on her left foot. Perhaps her feet are still swollen from the pregnancy and the ring no longer fits properly. Together they search for food, pecking at the grass and hopping around the planters in search of anything the soil can deliver. After some hunting and gathering, the he-bird takes off over the roof while she slips into the small tree to sit on the eggs.

After watching the two birds peck in the grass at bits of nothing yet again, my daughter and I decided they needed our savoir faire food-gathering skills. In the overnight we had had a rare downpour of rain, and so we were confident that a few pokes in the soft soil would deliver a squirmy earthworm for the husband and wife. However, my worm-locating attempts failed as several digs returned nothing. A large but manageable rock nearby triggered a thought. Perhaps lifting the rock would uncover some slimy creatures, high in protein and void of all trans fat. I turned over the rock, and there wiggling before my eyes was a lovely earthworm, the delight of every bird.

I plucked the worm from the moist dirt, tossed it onto the sidewalk in full view of Mr. and Mrs. Bird, slipped back into the house, and watched and waited for the bird to tweet with delight over my generous offering. My daughter called the play-by-play as we looked through the front window. "She's getting warmer. She sees the worm. She's hopping toward it — ooooh, she's getting warmer, nooo, she turned around and is getting colder now, and she's hopping away from the worm. Now she's freezing. Oooh, oooh, Mr. Bird sees the worm. He is right next to it. There he goes! He is getting warmer, and oh, he hopped away!"

Frustration mounted as we watched the two birds hop around the squiggly worm with no intentions of devouring the juicy creature. The worm continued to taunt the birds with jumps and turns. We informed both of them that they were stupid birds for ignoring the worm as we pulled it from the concrete path and tossed it back to safety.

Some people are like those birds. Let's take the ancient Israelites, for example. God promised them a land filled with milk and honey. All they had to do was obey his commands as they ventured through the wilderness. God provided them with manna from heaven. Their food actually appeared each morning like dew. All they had to do was pick up the manna and eat, but they didn't want that food. Even though the manna tasted sweet like honey and could be prepared many different ways, they hopped around ignoring God's blessing while grumbling on and on about wanting to return to slavery, where at least they could eat meat to their hearts' content. Preposterous!

If truth be told, I often ignore what God has placed before me — the blessings he has so graciously provided. I want something better, more up-to-date. Instead of a spacious, green backyard, I want the yard coated in concrete with an extravagant pool. Instead of my twelve-year-old car, which still runs well, I want the newer model. Rather than wear the clothes in my closet, I want more choices. I want to ditch my old bathroom and build one with a bigger shower and tub area. In place of my roof, I want to add a second story. Absurd! God still loves me and constantly reminds me that his grace and his mercy are sufficient.

The next time I went out to visit the birds, I set out sunflower seeds without the shells. I crushed them with my foot to make them manageable by beak. The seeds sat, woefully ignored. Mr. and Mrs. Bird pecked around in the grass as if the minuscule grass offerings were better than my delicious seeds. I'm done. I've had it. Those birds are on their own. If they don't want my help, well, then, they can just starve — either that, or they can just suffer through those tidbits of grass instead of fresh, juicy worms and roasted sunflower seeds. Stupid birds.

My God will meet all your needs according to the riches of his glory in Christ Jesus.

Philippians 4:19

saturating shock

My children wear "uniforms" that are not school ordered. They consist of the same two or three pairs of shorts and four to six stained and worn T-shirts weathered from lack of drawer time. The shirt colors vary only among brown, white, and black, and while blue is a faraway option, the hue must be light and powdery as opposed to deep and navy. The front logo must advertise a surf or skate company, and for my middle mister, the back of the shirt must be logo free. Gone are the days of dump truck-embellished T-shirts and denim carpenter-style shorts with an elastic waistband. Shopping with four children with finicky fashion tastes is exhausting; the good thing is that on those days, my shopping conveniently transcends into my morning cardio workout.

While shopping recently, I stumbled on a clearance rack filled with five-dollar shirts that met the "uniform" standards. Since I can never purchase a T-shirt without child approval, I gathered the brood around the circular rack and lifted hangers draped with T-shirts while anticipating approval. "Does this one work? How about this? Do you like this color blue? This one has skulls — you know the rule: no shirts with skulls." The queries flew as my window of opportunity was sliding shut and the kids' impatience inside a clothing store was widening. The metal hangers clanged each time I picked up one shirt and replaced it with another while assembling the thumbs-up pile on my stroller. The boys took turns meandering away, doing baseball slides on the slick concrete floor and hiding inside shirt racks, while my daughter deliberately dug through a discount rack and found a pair of ten-dollar denim shorts.

I left the store with a total of six shirts and one pair of shorts. Perhaps now everyone could wear a different shirt for one week without having to dig through the hamper for their soiled and wrinkled "favorite." I quickly returned home to start a load of laundry so that the newly purchased Ts would be ready to wear. While I was folding laundry, I held up the smallest shirt, a 4-T, and something caught my eye. There in the corner of my four-year-old's new shirt was a drawing of a skull-headed woman with wings — topless! My disappointment began with the fact that I had inadvertently purchased a shirt designed with skulls and [gulp] breasts. What on earth was a nude woman doing on a shirt for children? I called the store immediately to report my findings. Although I knew that teen shirts often have inappropriate drawings on the front, this T-shirt label was marked "Kids."

The store blamed the mishap on the buyer for the store. "Did you check the shirt before you bought it?" a salesgirl indignantly asked. In a curt tone I replied, "I didn't know I had to check a child's T-shirt for graphics of naked women." After voicing my disappointment on the buyer's message machine, I never received a return phone call. I could have stopped then and decided it wasn't going to be worth any more of the effort it took to get my money back or stop this from happening to other mothers of preschool children. I could have chalked the money loss up to good money gone bad and moved on, but I didn't. I immediately called the manufacturer and spoke to a lackadaisical twentysomething who was suffering from energy drink withdrawal. She thought the T-shirt was a case of the artist expressing his right to free speech. Honestly she couldn't understand why I thought it was such a big deal, but she reluctantly transferred my call to the head of the boy's department. After leaving another message, I never got a call back.

In addition to my attempts to contact a living person responsible for selling a preschool T-shirt with pornographic images, I emailed the local newspaper, television news station, and cable news channel. No one was shocked, let alone concerned — nor did they have a desire to delve into my headline story, "*Preschool Pornography: One Woman's Shocking Tale*."

Obviously the human shock level has become so saturated that inappropriate incidences are now passé. Two thousand years ago a woman committed adultery. The consequence for such an offense was stoning. The peers of this woman gathered around her, each bending down to gather a stone. Jesus enters the scene and questions the drama that is transpiring. When the Jewish leaders ask Jesus what they should do, he simply states, "Let any one of you who is without sin be the first to throw a stone at her" (John 8:7). The stones dropped to the ground, one by one, like heavy raindrops on cement. A stoning? For adultery? How inhumane and preposterous! What would they have done with preschool pornography?

Although many didn't think my outrage had warrant, I had to do something. Sitting on the telephone for any length of time attempting to find the appropriate person to contact was draining, yet sitting on my hands wasn't an option. Jesus calls us to be different, abnormal in character compared to the world, and to fight for what we believe is right, just, and pure. He calls us to battle the Enemy and his destructive army, to do better — better than shrugging our shoulders and rolling our eyes.

Eventually the gentleman from the manufacturer called

and left a message that voiced deep concern, regret, and sadness. The graphic designer who let this image escape his computer had since left the company. Shortly thereafter, I received a box in the mail containing a pair of jeans, four T-shirts, one hooded sweatshirt, and two long-sleeved T-shirts, all of which were brown, black, or white and didn't contain any skulls or naked ladies — and at no cost.

> *Let us not become weary in doing good, for at the proper time we will reap a harvest if we do not give up.*
>
> *Galatians 6:9*

persnickety

I made the mistake of feeding into the finicky fits of our firstborn child and her issues with certain types of food. Vegetables have always been a big no, yet she will devour a can filled with green peas in seconds flat. However, each pea must be evenly coated in butter and salt. Her bagged lunch must only contain a peanut butter sandwich on bread without crust, and the only chips she will eat are triangularly shaped and cheesy. While spaghetti gets her approval, the sauce must contain ground beef and never sausage.

I vigorously claimed, "I didn't know any better!" and "She was my first!" and solemnly swore to the family that the rest of my children would eat whatever I placed on their plates.

The three boys eat whatever is not moving and occasionally some things that are. In addition, one of them could lick the top of his hamburger and the others would gleefully take a bite, unaffected by the party of mouth germs resting on the bun. They also have no concern for the five-second rule. All items of food dropped on the ground, street, floorboard, tile, or sidewalk are as good as tasty. A fast, hard blast of mouth air to blow away unwanted dirt morsels from the piece of food ensures cleanliness and an "all clear" signal for consumption.

Recently we took the family to a restaurant to celebrate my birthday. Since I had filled a small suitcase with seven different types of electronic devices, Play-Doh, and enough stickers to wallpaper a small building, they behaved. The server complimented the kids on how well they cleaned their plates and then launched into a story about a family who had recently sat at one of her tables. The parents were trying to decide where to go on vacation. Since their children were such fussy eaters, they would have to find a spot that served the type of food their children would eat. Uzbekistan was probably out of the question, even though it has densely packed tombs that fastidious children could explore.

She also mentioned that one of the children launched into a mild freak-out when one of her chicken chunks touched a pile of white rice. Oh my! I would have put the chicken and rice in a blender and made her drink it through a straw. That child was obviously unfamiliar with a character trait called gratitude — either that, or she was suffering from an onslaught of self-centeredness coupled with an extreme case of spoiledness.

Opposite the girl lacking gratitude was King David. He was everything grateful. King David also had good looks, warrior skills, strong leadership qualities, and was a master harp player. Serenading women at dusk was quite likely out of the question for David. Harps are cumbersome and don't travel well.

Many of the psalms are written by David. While David was in the melting pot of remorse and concern with each wrong move, begging God for forgiveness and pleading for protection from oncoming enemies, he wrote songs of thankfulness and praise to God. In spite of his struggles and misfortune, he worshiped and repeatedly spoke prayers of devotion to God.

To this day, my daughter could only survive on a desolate, snow-covered mountaintop if someone was able to deliver chicken strips, French fries, and Coke and if no one else touched her food or took a sip of her drink. Thankfully, her food tastes have finally expanded to include more variety. However, on Thanksgiving, she will only eat the turkey if she can locate a slice underneath a pool of ketchup.

Give thanks in all circumstances; for this is God's will for you in Christ Jesus.

1 Thessalonians 5:18

operation hazmat

I begrudge housecleaning. I don't mind picking up the clut-
ter, but deep cleaning annoys me. I mutter words under my
breath as I scrub the stove and dust the furniture — words
that shouldn't be spoken louder than a mutter. I complain
about the fact that I should be spending time engaging in
a feral game of Go Fish with my children rather than slow
dancing with bleach and furniture polish.

In a perfect world my children would rise early, sit
around the dining room table, enjoy a hearty breakfast of
eggs (cooked to order) and bacon, with biscuits and gravy,
and would then march off without complaining to do their
daily chores. However, when I do attempt to dole out a list
of chores, the end result for chore completion is a C minus
or D plus instead of an A minus or B plus. If only bed

making and vacuuming made for a home that is filled with sparkle, the kids would receive an A plus, because my oldest loves to vacuum.

Housecleaning was raised to an unthinkable level when my mother became ill. A sudden onset of the flu had her doing things in places you shouldn't be doing those things. Imagine, if you will, that your two-year-old has the flu and has been throwing up all night. Multiply that times a 150-pound woman in her sixties, and you have an idea of what I was about to face. She was desperate, and she needed my services.

I arrived at her house armed with spray bleach and paper towels. A green, plastic yard bag covered my top half, in which I had cut out holes for my arms. If my feet had been small enough to fit into my son's red rubber firefighter rain boots, I would have shoved them on. I knew enough to avoid wearing flip-flops, though, and opted for old sneakers.

The situation was grave, yet I was well prepared. Through heavy mouth breathing, in order to avoid any and all smells attempting to permeate my nostrils, I scrubbed, cursed, washed, grumbled, mopped, complained, scoured, mumbled, rubbed, and objected. The scent of a freshly sanitized home eventually bulldozed through the stench, and my job was complete.

I may have grumbled enough that day to cover the next nine years, and I prayed that my mother's health would

spilt milk

remain stable indefinitely. Finding joy in that situation was quite a challenge.

Paul, one of Jesus' apostles, had more reason to gripe than anyone. Paul expelled a demon from a slave girl who was earning a fair amount of money for her master by fortune-telling. Why he didn't just have her sell fortune cookies from a corner kiosk is beyond me.

Because this girl could no longer tell the future, Paul was accused of opposing Roman customs and was thrown into jail along with his friend Silas. Paul and Silas sat in the midst of darkness, spiders, stone walls and rocks for pillows. With their feet bound in stocks, Paul and Silas begin praying and singing praises to God.

I'd be lying if I said I'd be doing the same thing. After collapsing into a heap of tears and depression, I'd be asking God, "Why, why, why?" I don't do well in isolation — unless the room includes a king-sized bed, a full-body massage masseuse, turndown service, and an endless supply of delicious caffeinated beverages.

Although I can never escape housecleaning and I may never wake up in the morning and shout, "Housecleaning rocks!" I can turn on worship music the next time I'm doing chores in order to change my outlook. After all, I do love a house that smells like pine cleaner, but only slightly less than I love a gigantic bowl of salty tortilla chips with a side of mild salsa.

I have learned to be content whatever the circumstances.

Philippians 4:11

hunger pangs

Given the unappeasable appetites of four children, I have succumbed to purchasing overpriced convenience food they can grab on the go or prepare for themselves. I have considered the off chance that each child's culinary craving is due in part to the fact that he or she is hosting a six-foot-long tapeworm, but the doctor says no.

Since I'm not an organic-buying mom who avoids all foods containing red dye, corn syrup, and trans fat, or who only serves beef from cows that eat soy-flavored, multivitamin infused hay and drink bottled springwater from stalactite caves, anything goes. Some of the items I'm about to reveal as foods I actually feed my children without any level of guilt may bring on nausea or an unceasing twitch. Consider yourself warned.

Any canned pasta with a shelf life of one year whose contents can be warmed in the microwave in thirty seconds suffices as breakfast, lunch, or dinner. Drinkable yogurt with enough sugar to jump-start a hibernating bear is another favorite. I know that yogurt contains something cultured — funguslike — and is good for children. Pockets of pastry dough stuffed with pizza sauce and cheese are quick and easy, and yellow foam cakes packed full of white mystery cream can sustain a nuclear war and make for a tasty treat.

My all-time favorite, number one convenience food is microwave popcorn — movie-theater style, blasted with pseudobutter. My children thought that the microwave popcorn was the greatest taste in the world until the day my mother made them "real" popcorn. She dragged out the black-bottomed cauldron circa 1912, poured in the oil, popped all the kernels, and then coated each plump kernel with salt and gobs of real melted butter. Can you smell it?

My kid's short trip to "popcorn heaven" has created great tension between my kids and me. Not only did I birth them, nurse them, and have the A cup bra as proof, but they now want to know why I don't make real popcorn like Grandma does. So I lie and tell them, "You cannot make great popcorn without the pot, and Grandma has the only pot on the planet, possibly in the universe." I suppose I'll get the pot when she dies. However, my mother knows full well that she is never to die — ever.

I wish that being a Christian was convenient and easy, that going to church and making sure to pray at least once a day sufficed for a genuine relationship with Jesus. However, I know there is more to leading the Christian life than that.

Daily I feel the tension between trying to please God by being the kind of woman he has created me to be and trying to tame my character flaws. Being a mom of children ages preschool through PMS seriously tests my character, yet the more I attempt to remain in him and pray often, the easier it becomes to walk with the Lord and remain in him. God is more concerned with how I react to difficult circumstances than with how many times I say a prayer — although he loves to hear my prayers too.

Looking inward and documenting the areas in which I fall short of God's ideal for me is a humiliating yet necessary step in becoming a better person. Thankfully, no neon sign hovers over my head, spelling out each moral error. When I am painfully honest, I acknowledge that I am sarcastic, critical, impatient, and selfish — and that's just the first four flaws on my list of many. God still has a lot of work to do with me. As hard as I try, I continue to fail.

If I have any hope of becoming more like Jesus, I'm going to have to put in much more effort than I do in providing healthy snacks for my children. Becoming a woman of God doesn't come microwave fast but involves a slow simmer over time. Plus, we all know that anything cooked in the microwave doesn't taste as good as homemade food — especially popcorn.

> *"I am the vine; you are the branches. If you remain in me and I in you, you will bear much fruit; apart from me you can do nothing."*
>
> *John 15:5*

stupid words

All families have their own vocabulary preferences for what is and is not allowed to be said in their homes. While the neighbor boys call the bodily function blast that erupts from your backside a *fart*, we use the word *toot*. That hunk of flesh everyone uses to sit on is in our house called a *butt*, while other families choose words like *rump*, *hiney*, *behind*, and *fanny*.

While all cusswords are out of the question, disrespectful slang words like *pimp* and *homey* have no place in our home either. In addition, no child, teen or otherwise, may approach the kitchen and ask, "Yo, what's for dinner, home chick?" In these cases I would reply, "Nottalotta, home nugget!" — and that child would experience an indefinite time-out.

spilt milk

There are three very common words that my kids and most children are not allowed to say until they are at least in high school: *stupid*, *shut up*, and *idiot*. Since I happen to use these words on occasion, correcting my children's use of them makes for a difficult situation.

The fact is that there are certain times when these three words are appropriate. A fly buzzing around your head is most definitely stupid. Stupid may also be used to describe a jackrabbit that attempted to play Red Rover with speeding cars in the middle of an intersection and ended up as roadkill.

Black widow spiders are stupid, especially when they give my children nightmares. All can agree that running out of gas is stupid, mainly when it occurs on the freeway in downtown Los Angeles, where you need a bulletproof vest just to enter a fast-food restaurant.

Using the word *idiot* may be less acceptable, but at the same time it's the only word that will suffice in certain situations. Feeling like an idiot — and saying so out loud after you offer a baby wipe to a friend for dirt removal on her neck and the dirt happens to be a birthmark — gets the OK. Also, during a pedicure, when the kind aesthetician approaches and relentlessly insists that you need an upper-lip wax, thinking out loud, "Am I an idiot for not noticing the caterpillar sleeping above my lip?" would most assuredly be OK. In that case, the aesthetician would just nod and return with the essential arsenal for hair removal.

The exclamation *shut up* has long been in my vocabulary as what I say when I'm surprised by something someone tells me. For instance, "Yeah, I have twelve cats, three rabbits, a pony, and two goats" would receive a resounding "Shut up!" as in "No way!" Same meaning, different expression. I work the graveyard shift as a wordsmith, and so muttering "shut up" under my breath to the parrots as their caws penetrate my open bedroom window at 6:00 a.m. is also great word usage. No parrot would be outwardly offended — or inwardly offended, for that matter.

I believe that when Jesus entered the temple courts, he may have used the word *idiots* — though I can't find that exact wording in any Bible. As the story goes, there were masses of people buying and selling items in the temple, the house of God. They weren't selling weekly devotionals, podcasted sermons to be downloaded, or daily prayer suggestions on strips of paper neatly tucked inside plastic loaves of bread. They were selling livestock.

Outraged by this profane use of God's temple, Jesus overturned the tables where the money changers and dove sellers were sitting saying, "My house will be called a house of prayer, but you are making it 'a den of robbers'" (Matthew 21:13). I'm guessing that the sentence started with "You idiots!" but was lost in translation. However, I never went to seminary and only know one word in Aramaic.

Our words can have a great effect on people. I'll bet all

of us can remember a time when someone said something unkind to us, and those words became etched on the stone tablets of our memories. As easily as we can remember the hurtful words, we also can remember words of encouragement, affirmation, and edification. These words change our lives for the better and strengthen our core being. Some of these life-affirming words include, "Great job!" "You're so helpful!" "I love your encouragement!" "You are so special!" "You're a great friend!" "I'm proud of you!" These words build us up and also bring glory to God.

While I continue to work on my words, my children keep pushing the proverbial envelope as they seek innovative and assorted ways to suitably use the infamous three — *stupid*, *shut up*, and *idiot*. In a final, last-ditch effort, my youngest recently questioned, "Can I say that the Devil is stupid?" Through a stifled grin, I replied, "Yes, the Devil is stupid."

May these words of my mouth and this meditation
of my heart
be pleasing in your sight,
LORD, my Rock and my Redeemer.

Psalm 19:14

when i grow up

When I was ten, I was the head cartoonist of the *Saranac Street Gazette*, circulation 3. I had high hopes of becoming an artist who specialized in illustrating children's books. My mother supported and encouraged my artistic endeavors by purchasing the tools needed to practice my drawing skills — a drawing pad, soft lead pencils, and a gum eraser.

For my more serious artistic attempts, she bought me watercolors and brushes and, upon completion, hung each painted canvas and penciled masterpiece on the refrigerator for all to admire. She even encouraged me to enter a Halloween poster contest. Much to my dismay, my haunted house poster received honorable mention from the judges — not first, second, or even third, but honorable mention, which is code for "your poster was terrible, but we had to acknowledge your entry."

When I decided to be a vet instead of an artist, my mom's encouragement was stellar. Our home was never void of a pet dog on which to practice my veterinarian skills, and in case I got tired of chasing my dog around the yard in an effort to enlist his help by making him a "patient," there were a plethora of stuffed animals on which to practice.

By the time I reached high school, the veterinarian idea vanished. Since I got a D plus in Algebra I and a D in Algebra II — and discovering that excelling in math is a requirement to becoming a vet — I quickly squelched any thought of helping animals beyond feeding and walking them. Throughout the roller-coaster ride of my various career choices, my mom was my constant encourager. She never once rolled her eyes at me.

In college I settled on a major in graphic design. I had the phenomenal ability of copying anything I saw — verbatim — but I lacked skill in developing a design from scratch. So when my professor asked us to come up with an original design for a painting, I panicked. In total desperation and lacking any original thoughts, I squeezed gobs of acrylic paint from tubes and slathered an array of color over white canvas. The abstract approach worked — an A grade appeared on the back of my painting. An A is always encouraging, yet it couldn't sustain a career.

The proverbial handwriting was on the wall, so during the last semester of my senior year, I decided to become an elementary school teacher, even though I was graduating with a degree in art and would have to continue my education.

My mother never shook her head in frustration, told me I was crazy for changing my mind after I had already graduated, or insisted that I clean houses and walk dogs during the summer in order to pay for the additional education needed to get teaching credentials. Instead, she was thrilled that I was following in her teaching footsteps, and she continued to be an encouragement.

Paul, an apostle of Jesus, was an encourager extraordinaire. He wrote letters to Timothy that gave him guidance and support as he preached and taught. This wasn't an easy job, since Timothy was young, not an apostle, and perhaps not well respected. No one was fixing him fancy dinners and hanging on every word that fell from his lips.

Knowing Timothy's struggles, Paul wrote to him and reminded him that he had great gifts from God for ministry and that Paul loved him as a son. "Don't let anyone look down on you because you are young," Paul wrote, "but set an example for the believers in speech, in conduct, in love, in faith and in purity" (1 Timothy 4:12). Who wouldn't appreciate getting a letter or a text message that was this encouraging?

Although I had an encouraging role model in my life, I

don't always encourage others like I should. To help me be more proactive in the compliment department, God graciously gives me what I call "brain taps" — a way of reminding me to voice compliments that have been percolating in my brain. Some of these "brain taps" include telling a neighbor that his house looks beautiful or telling a friend that her children behaved fabulously while visiting at our home.

I especially love to tell my children that I'm proud of them or how much I appreciate when they want to try a new sport or stifle a burp at the dinner table, or when they get a D in algebra after trying their absolute best. God is ultimately the great encourager, and when we remember to encourage others, we are imitating him.

Oh, by the way. Would anyone like a colorful abstract painting to hang in their home or a poster of a haunted house? I happen to have some extras.

Encourage one another and build each other up,
just as in fact you are doing.

1 Thessalonians 5:11

scoot scooter!

I read somewhere that dogs can smell fear. I'm in the clear, since I fear only one type of dog: Pit bulls. I know, I know, pit bulls are misunderstood. They are really great with children and are as gentle as a caterpillar, right?

I encounter many dogs while I'm jogging through our neighborhood. They are typically leashed, friendly, and accompanied by an owner. If I ever come across a dog that is without an owner, they will usually ignore me and find a shrub with a better scent. My non-fear, outdoor jog smell evidently doesn't entice stray dogs. For that I'm grateful.

My fate turned one day as I approached two dogs — one large, one small — both unleashed and happy to be cruising along the sidewalk without an owner in sight. I patted them on the back as I passed by. Much to my dismay, both dogs began to follow me. I stopped for a moment to check their collars for tags and noticed that the bigger one's tag had a phone number and that his name was Scooter. The smaller dog had a collar but no tag. Since I had no way of contacting the owners, I, being mobile phone free, continued on my jog.

Immediately the smaller dog walked in the opposite direction as if he was following a GPS navigation system back to his house. The bigger dog, Scooter, started to follow me. Frustrated, I pretended to find a ball in a nearby bush, yelled, "Get the ball, Scooter!" and watched him run in the direction of the invisible ball. I resumed my uphill jog, satisfied that I was finally alone. After a few paces, I heard a pitter-patter noise behind me. I turned to look and saw that Scooter was back, hot on my heels.

Mistakenly I figured I could outrun him, and so I took off at an astounding eight miles per hour instead of five. He followed, so I darted through some trees, hoping to escape his golden fur, but he continued to follow. I yelled at Scooter to leave me alone, but he never listened. "I don't want you" I shouted, while he continued to jog alongside me. However ingenious, my dog-ditching efforts were falling short.

I just wanted to jog. I didn't want to be responsible for a dog, his stamina, or his safety. Cars slowed to a crawl as Scooter sauntered into the street while I yelled to the drivers, "He's not my dog! He's following me!" I didn't want anyone to think I was carelessly running a dog without a leash and letting him meander into the street every now and again just for kicks.

Breathless and exhausted, I stopped at the top of the hill and leaned down to have a talk with Scooter. "Unless you have a bottle of water tucked inside your fur, please stop following me and go home. I don't want you." He ignored my demand and began to walk faster as I jogged away.

On the last quarter mile of my jog, Scooter fell in an exhausted heap on the sidewalk that led up to a blue-and-white house. As I passed him, I cheered, "You shouldn't have followed me, Scooter." I felt free, elated, as I turned the corner and disappeared from Scooter's view. I had finally detoured his dangling tongue and persistent pursuit. My conscience was somewhat assuaged because I knew that, since he wore a collar with a tag, someone on the street would place a phone call, and Scooter would eventually get to his house. He wasn't my responsibility.

As soon as I was out of Scooter's sight, a mantra began in my head: "Do the right thing. Do the right thing." I didn't want to do the right thing, I was on a time limit, and I wanted to finish my jog, not worry about "Scooter the stalking dog." However, the idea that I should do the right thing wouldn't leave me. I cut my run short, and when I got home, I quickly got in my car and drove the three blocks to where Scooter had stopped to rest and forced him into my car. I drove home, deposited Scooter into my backyard, gave him a bowl with water, and called the number on his tag.

spilt milk

God is great at pursuing his children. As I look back at the times in my life when I wanted to leave God at home while I overindulged in cocktails with college friends or snuck into R-rated movies as a preteen, God continued to draw me back to him. When I sought out a spouse without prayer and outside of God's will, my marriage failed. When I faked a Christian walk on Sundays and strayed all week, God continued to reveal himself to me and to remind me of his love for me. When I fell in a heap at his feet, his perseverance prevailed and his concern for my well-being was apparent. When I zigged, God zigged. When I snuck behind a bush, he followed. When I told him to leave me alone, he told me he wanted to be near me. I'm indebted to God for never giving up on his quest for my heart.

Scooter's persistence paid off. Not only did he receive a nice long walk, but he slaked his thirst with cool water, was treated to a can of doggie beef stew, and then fell asleep in the shade of a tree. When Scooter's happy owners picked him up, they were relieved to have him back with their family and thanked me profusely for my good deed. "It was my pleasure!" I announced, winking at my husband. After all, I love dogs, even Scooter the stalking dog — now that he is home.

"This is what the Sovereign LORD says: I myself will search for my sheep and look after them."

Ezekiel 34:11

acknowledgments

Thanks to my children, Maddy, Zac, Ty, Carson,
who never fail to provide fodder for my stories.

Thanks to my mother, Emily Chumchal,
who not only provided huge encouragement but knew
when to tell me that a story wasn't funny enough
and when to remind me that I needed
a refresher course on comma usage.

Thanks to Zondervan and my editor Andy Meisenheimer,
who took a chance on my writing and believed
I had something worth publishing.

Share Your Thoughts

With the Author: Your comments will be forwarded to the author when you send them to *zauthor@zondervan.com*.

With Zondervan: Submit your review of this book by writing to *zreview@zondervan.com*.

Free Online Resources at
www.zondervan.com/hello

 Zondervan AuthorTracker: Be notified whenever your favorite authors publish new books, go on tour, or post an update about what's happening in their lives.

 Daily Bible Verses and Devotions: Enrich your life with daily Bible verses or devotions that help you start every morning focused on God.

 Free Email Publications: Sign up for newsletters on fiction, Christian living, church ministry, parenting, and more.

 Zondervan Bible Search: Find and compare Bible passages in a variety of translations at www.zondervanbiblesearch.com.

 Other Benefits: Register yourself to receive online benefits like coupons and special offers, or to participate in research.